Emmanuel's Book

9-92

To Melanie,

With much love,

BANTAM NEW AGE BOOKS

This important imprint includes books in a variety of fields and disciplines and deals with the search for meaning, growth and change. They are books that circumscribe our times and our future.

Ask your bookseller for the books you have missed.

Emmanuel's Book

*A manual
for living comfortably
in the cosmos*

Compiled by
**Pat Rodegast and
Judith Stanton**

Illustrated by
Roland Rodegast

Introduction by
Ram Dass

BANTAM BOOKS
NEW YORK · TORONTO · LONDON · SYDNEY · AUCKLAND

*This edition contains the complete text
of the original hardcover edition.*
NOT ONE WORD HAS BEEN OMITTED.

EMMANUEL'S BOOK

*A Bantam Book / published by arrangement with
Friends' Press*

PRINTING HISTORY

*Friends' edition published November 1985
6 printings through March 1988
Bantam edition / March 1987*

*New age and the accompanying figure design as well as the
statement ''the search for meaning, growth and change'' are
trademarks of Bantam Books.*

ISBN 0-553-34387-4

Published simultaneously in the United States and Canada

---

*Bantam Books are published by Bantam Books, a division of Bantam
Doubleday Dell Publishing Group, Inc. Its trademark, consisting of the
words ''Bantam Books'' and the portrayal of a rooster, is Registered in
U.S. Patent and Trademark Office and in other countries. Marca
Registrada. Bantam Books, 666 Fifth Avenue, New York, New York
10103.*

PRINTED IN THE UNITED STATES OF AMERICA

O   15   14   13   12   11

Dedicated
to the image that each soul holds
within its own human consciousness
and to the memory
of the Light that it follows,
of the Being that it yearns to become
and of the Truth that it already is.

Contents

Prologue
Emmanuel

The gifts I wish to give you
are my deepest love,
the safety of truth,
the wisdom of the universe
and the reality of God.

With these four things, nothing will deter you.
You will follow your hearts
swiftly to your destination,
which is Home.

I know there is confusion and doubt
and what appears to be chaos.
Can you see
that beneath these surface shadows
there is eternal Light?

This earth plane
is neither the beginning nor the end
of your existence.
It is simply a step, a schoolroom.

My friends, let me impress upon you
how solidly
you are planted in eternity,
how brilliantly
you can shine in your own physical world,
how possible
it all is,
how beautifully
the Plan is designed.

In God's Plan no soul is alone.
No soul is ever lost.

Introduction:
My Friend Emmanuel

Again and again in spiritual texts one is enjoined to seek out the company of the holy, that is those whose lives are committed to God. I, for one, readily admit that I am addicted to such beings, for reflected in them I can see the spiritual aspects of myself and of the world around me, aspects which in the marketplace are so often veiled by 'this' and 'that'.

From my Guru, Neem Karoli Baba, I received encouragement to take teachings wherever I could find them and then to trust my intuitive heart to cull the teachings which would be useful from those which were irrelevant or potentially harmful. His support enabled me to open wide and receive rich returns from a great variety of different traditions and sources. Whether through the written words of such beings as Lao Tzu, the Buddha, the Third Chinese Patriarch, the Christ, Kabir, Ramana Maharshi, The Baal Shem Tov, Ramakrishna, etc., or the darshans of such noble souls as Grandpa Joe of the Taos Pueblo, Ananda Mayee Ma, Kalu Rinpoche of the Kargyu Tibetan Sect, Father Demasius of the Benedictines, Lama Govinda, Sayadaw U Pandita of the Therevadans, etc., I have profited greatly. These voices of compassionate wisdom are what the Therevadan Buddhists refer to as 'Kalayan Mita' or Spiritual Friends: beings whom met along the way provide guidance and support for one's spiritual journey. Emmanuel, for me, is another of these voices. It is a priviledge to be able to introduce him to you and to share his teachings with you.

I first heard Emmanuel on WBAI in New York City. Actually, I heard Pat Rodegast reporting what Emmanuel was saying. She had been in contact for some time with this being whom she referred to as Emmanuel. She could contact him at will through meditative tuning and could hear him clearly though others around her could not. To each question asked by Lex Hixon, the host of the radio program, Pat relayed Emmanuel's response.

Listening to that radio show, what I was most struck by was Emmanuel's charm and old-world courtliness, his humor, eloquence, directness, 'hip'ness, and the fact that his responses evoked intuitive trust in me. By the end of the show a number of questions of both a personal and general nature had arisen in my mind and I asked Judith Stanton, who had introduced me to Emmanuel through that program, to try to arrange an interview for me with Pat and Emmanuel.

The interview was held in a quiet meditative room looking out on a garden. As we settled in, Pat started a tape recorder so that I could have a record of our conversation. Pat started to describe colors which she saw as associated with me. In the middle of this description she said, "Emmanuel wants to say something. He is saying......" and then she reported Emmanuel's comments about the colors, and we were off and running.

I had no sense of Pat being 'possessed' by Emmanuel. Rather, Pat remained very much herself, but willingly conveyed Emmanuel's words in a way that indicated that it was a relaxed, light, and quite delightful friendship that she shared with Emmanuel. The differences between them were very noticeable. Most obviously, there were marked differences in sentence structure, linguistic patterns, and choice of words. But more subtly, there was a vibratory difference as well. At first I barely noticed this subtle quality. However, in later interviews this vibratory space came to have as profound and significant a value for me as Emmanuel's words.

In that initial interview Pat also described other images she was seeing. Among them: "I see you very involved in playing a game. There is a feeling of tremendous excitement. You are sitting hunched over the game board in intense concentration." Then she said, "Emmanuel, help me because I feel there is something more there and I can't...."

Emmanuel: "You take great joy in life, in the game of life. That is not degrading it. There is a charismatic excitement."

I laughed as I recalled the numerous times in lectures when I had quoted Leo from Herman Hesse's *Journey to the East* when he says, "Don't you see that's just what life is...a beautiful game?"

Pat then added, "There is no opponent that I can see."

Emmanuel: "You have already long since identified the opponent and removed it by accepting it into your own being as the manifestation of yourself." He was right in that observation. But he didn't let me rest on my laurels. He was quick to point out that I still hadn't reconciled these forces within myself, and was still plagued by the dualistic separation between divinity and humanity which underlay my fears of my human condition. "There is divinity in all things," he pointed out," "and in order to find the divinity one must work with the material at hand. . . . In the clay of the pot is the truth of God."

He returned again and again to my suspicions of my passions and my fear of surrendering to my humanity. He kept reassuring me that my human desires were very much part of my spiritual journey and that through them rather than in spite of them I would find God.

As I reread the transcript of that first interview I see a confusion in our conversation that was only resolved as I came to recognize that Emmanuel was not speaking to me as I was used to being addressed. Most people, even those of us who acknowledge that we are souls incarnated in bodies and personalities, speak to one another as ego. . .as a psychological entity. The reason it took me time to acclimate to Emmanuel's conversation was because Emmanuel was addressing me as a fellow soul, not as an ego. After all, he did not identify himself with a particular timespace configuration and thus did not identify me in that way, either.

This form of address at first seemed quaint, and I kept trying to translate it into ego address, assuming that he was speaking to me as a psychological being trying to awaken. Slowly, however, as I surrendered into the identity of a soul who was passing through an incar-nation, the conversation not only became clear, but I realized that this unfamiliar form of address was, in itself, a liberating factor.

Over time I have come to be quite comfortable being

with Emmanuel as a fellow soul, and have all but forgotten the unusual (for me) fact that I am speaking with
someone who is not embodied on the plane of reality
that is so familiar to my senses. From time to time those
of us around Emmanuel speculate as to 'where' he is
or 'who' he is. Emmanuel does not seem eager to satisfy
our idle curiosity, however, and offers only the sketch-
iest of clues:

"I am spirit and you are spirit. I have a body and
so do you. Mine is slightly altered by the altering
of my consciousness."

"It is not such a big step between your reality and
mine. There is a belief that you who are in physical
form are the only solid existence in the universe.
This is clearly not true. We all have our physical
reality. Mine may not be as photogenic as yours,
but it certainly exists."

"You are where I am. I am where you are. And the
physical dimensions of height, and depth and
width have no reality at all. If you were to remove
the spectacles of human limitation, you and I
would face each other in perfect equality."

"You and I are walking the same path. We are
seeking truth and our souls are yearning back
towards the One God. All of us are growing within
our own realm. There it is."

He notes at one point, "I am no longer subject to the
tyranny of the calendar and the clock." And in speaking
of death, he says, "I, myself, am a product of the
afterdeath experience." Regarding his function, he says,
"Those of us who no longer need to be human exist
in a realm of consciousness in which we are available

to guide and to teach."

Ramakrishna, the great Indian Saint said of spiritual transmission, "When the flower blooms the bees come uninvited." Certainly with Emmanuel this seemed to be the case. Over the past few years the number of people seeking workshops and interviews with Emmanuel has increased dramatically. Pat and Judith, who was transcribing many of the interviews, noted how often the same questions were repeated and how Emmanuel had to repeat the same material again and again. So an effort was made to collate the answers to the most oft asked questions and photocopy them. This was the way in which this book was born. Subsequently we saw the desirability of broadening the scope of material covered beyond that which emerged in individual interviews. So we asked Emmanuel if he would be willing to entertain sets of prepared questions for a book. He was delighted to participate, pointing out that that was, after all, what he was there for.

We commenced a series of meetings with five of us present. Besides Pat and Judith, there was Roland, myself, and, of course, Emmanuel. The meetings were joyous. The chance to explore the ponderables and imponderables of the spiritual journey with Emmanuel provided clarity which cut through confusions which had long plagued one or another of us. However, the joy came not only from the words, but, from time to time, from the rich compassionate healing silence that would permeate the room and the hearts therein gathered. Again and again it seemed that Emmanuel would use words to point us in a direction and then gently prod us to go beyond the intellect and into the silence of our intuitive hearts, where separation disappeared and knowledge gave way to wisdom.

This balance of word and silence, form and formless, relationship and the unity which transcends relationship was such an integral part of the teachings and brought us such joy, that we have sought a format for Emmanuel's book that might invite you who share this material to use the words as a diving board from which to dive into your own inner silence where you and Emmanuel can share that which is beyonds words. So we have used space along with the words, hopefully not to be ignored, but rather to suggest that you punctuate the readings with quiet meditative reflection.

I have been asked again and again when presenting the Emmanuel material in lectures whether I really believe that Emmanuel is a separate being from Pat or whether he is another part of Pat's personality with which she does not consciously identify. For Pat, of course, there isn't even a question. She clearly experiences Emmanuel as a separate entity in the same way she experiences the rest of us.

From my point of view as a psychologist, I allow for the theoretical possibility that Emmanuel is a deeper part of Pat. However, experientially, I know Emmanuel as quite separate in personality, language style and vibration from the way in which I know Pat. In the final analysis, what difference does it really make? What I treasure is the wisdom Emmanuel conveys as an essence spiritual friend. Beyond this his identity doesn't really matter. As Ramana Maharshi, a great Indian Saint pointed out, "God, Guru, and Self are One." This is reflected in most mystic traditions which enjoin the seeker to 'Know thyself and thou shalt know God.' So I see Emmanuel as a mirror, and possibly an identity with not only Pat's higher consciousness or true Self, but mine as well. Thus, I feel that I am speaking to another part of my own being that I still do not have easy access to because of the blinders of attachment.

Finally, Emmanuel's oft-repeated injunction to us to trust only those teachings from him or anyone else that feel intuitively right in our deepest heart is to me the final criterion and protection that we must apply in regard to any system, whatever its source. Cosmologies, by the nature of the metaphysics with which they deal, have no scientific or empirical base. We really must seek ultimate validation in our deepest being.

Emmanuel's friendship has deepened my faith in the spirit. With regard to a number of topics he has helped me to clarify my understanding and my ability to express that understanding. On numerous occasions in lectures when I was reaching for a way to explain a point of dharma, an appropriate phrase or an example of Emmanuel's would come to mind and tongue. In this way I have felt the grace of having a friend like Emmanuel.

Here are some of the topics in which Emmanuel has helped me to validate my intuitive understandings.

1. Emmanuel is not the least bit put off by darkness, negativity, evil, or sin...the bugaboos of humanity. These he points to as necessary components of the curriculum of incarnation. They are not errors nor do they reflect any lack of compassion of spirit. He encourages us to see life not as a prison but as a schoolroom; not as a battle but rather as a dance.

2. He reiterates again and again that there is nothing to fear in darkness either in life or in death. Confusion, doubt, chaos and crisis, anger, despair

and pain are all excellent conditions for growth. He is so persuasive that one is encouraged to look at one's fears and inner darkness in a different light ...more as reflections of the way our minds distort the light. He is unbending in his assertion that the roots of the universe are love and light and that every experience can serve to renew our appreciation of that fact.

3. Because Emmanuel speaks to us as fellow souls, he points to our life experiences as the result of our creative choice. He asserts that we are both the creator (soul) and the created (body, personality, etc.) He encourages us to accept the responsibility for our creation. By doing this we get free of the sense of victimization that comes from identifying only with the creation.

4. Emmanuel does not advocate a renunciation that involves any denial of our humanity. Quite the opposite. He encourages us to treat our humanity (desires, attachments, etc.) as clues to God's truth. He cautions against looking for higher truths elsewhere than in life itself. He suggests that God can be found in a wonderful belly laugh or watching a kitten at play. At one point one of the interviewees responded to a point Emmanuel had made by saying, "It's a beautiful thought, Emmanuel." To which Emmanuel replied, "The entire universe is a beautiful thought."

5. Being with Emmanuel one comes to appreciate the vast evolutionary context in which our lives are being lived. We see ourselves in a larger tapestry as part of the creative pulse that is God, a creativity that takes us into the darkness of the illusion of separateness, and then out of it back into Unity. And at each moment we are at just the right place

in the journey. As Emmanuel points out, "Who you are is a necessary step to being who you will be." And who we will be is not necessarily always in human form. He reminds us, and in fact is himself a testament that a human incarnation is neither the beginning nor the end of our path of re-awakening consciousness as souls.

6. Again and again Emmanuel reiterates how the darkness is a product of our intellect. He advises us that the preeminence of the judging, discriminating, polarizing intellect must give way to our heart and our intuition if we are to be privy to the higher wisdom. "The heart knows the soul better than the mind does."

7. Regarding the planet and its ecology, Emmanuel suggests that it is going through a transformation of a more profound sort than what we immediately perceive. These larger designs incorporate into themselves the chaos and lack of consciousness in world affairs which so concern us at the moment. He characterizes most political leaders as children who don't really 'know better.' They are sick with the cancer of society, which exists in some degree in each of us as well...namely the belief that violence born of greed, which in turn is born of fear, is stronger than love. In this cancerous belief, vulnerability and compassion are seen as weak and dangerous. And he suggests that humans are arrogant if they think that they can end the world at their whim. He says, "School cannot be dismissed so early. The bell will not ring." He cautions us not to wash our hands of the earth, and says, "It has many good years left."

8. Emmanuel speaks about death at length and from the refreshing perspective of the other side.

He points out that dying (the how and the when) is as much part of the soul's plan of incarnation as any other life experience. His characterization of the experience at the moment of death is quite delightful. He speaks of it being like "taking off a tight shoe," or "going out the door of a rather stuffy room." He says, "There is something remarkably refreshing and educating about dying." and he reassures us that "it is *absolutely safe*." In speaking about the after death experience, he says that the difference between souls that has been reflected in the individual differences in their life incarnation continues to be reflected in the diverse experiences after death. His remarks give us a context for the many disparate reports that we have about what it's like 'on the other side.'

9. Emmanuel speaks about such other topics as sexuality, abortion, relationships, truth, religions and rituals, extra-terrestial beings, etc. To these topics so often surrounded with turgid and muddy reflection he brings a lightness and clarity that provides refreshingly constructive perspective.

In all of this there is really nothing *new*. It's all been said before somewhere or other in the mystic literature. Emmanuel himself points this out and says that we are not in need of any new information. We already have everything we need. But though it's all been said before, we need to hear it again and again, and to hear it in terms appropriate to the current context or 'zeitgeist' in which we find ourselves. Emmanuel does that wonderfully well.

I can only hope for you that Emmanuel will serve you as a spiritual friend as well as he has served me.

In love,

Ram Dass

Living with Emmanuel

I would like to share with you what it is like for me to live with Emmanuel.

Some fourteen years ago, during my TM meditations, I became distracted by inner visions, which continued despite my efforts to suppress them. I finally decided to allow these visions their space. From that moment everything in my life changed, as the romantic novels say.

At first I felt I might be hallucinating. That was very frightening. So I began to look for what others had to say about such things. I read a lot and attended lectures and classes in anything and everthing that might remotely relate to these experiences. I entered therapy, joined a spiritual community, fluctuated between resisting and flowing with it, enjoying and denying it. Eventually, through my searching, self-clearing, and maybe just familiarity, the confusion about these visions gave way to a degree of comfort, fascination, and even enjoyment.

In the course of this exploration I became aware of how strong a force fear had been in my life. Nameless fear, for the most part. Fear of so many things, including, at first, the visions. But once I became comfortable with them I began to look to these visions for guidance in alleviating my other fears. For example, flying has always terrified me. It seems quite remarkable to me that now that I have opened to these visionary experiences, particularly the ones involving Emmanuel, and tuned myself to their wisdom, I can actually enjoy an entire airplane flight. I see now that what initially drove me to meditation, and then to explore these visions, was fear. . .and the courage to overcome that fear, I am reminded to say. I had an intense longing to bring proof to my children, as well as to the child in me, that the world is safe. I didn't want my children to be as frightened as I was. It may seem an odd justification for opening a spiritual door, but it worked. It propelled me onto a spiritual journey, in the course of which I found my fears subsiding. Now, gratefully, I can say that I know that the universe is safe as do my now-grown children.

As my apprehension abated, love moved in. The first time I saw Emmanuel, some two years after the initial visual breakthrough, he appeared, as he still does, as a being of golden light. At first he would seem to be standing to my right, just within my line of vision but not predominant in any way. Gradually he moved more and more to the center of my inner vision so that in a week's time he was clearly standing directly in front of me. I asked who he was. "I am Emmanuel," he replied . "Will you be with me?" I queried. His answer was a simple and sweet "Yes." Thus, our work together began.

At first I simply enjoyed sitting in meditation and being with him for, you see, the most important thing is not what I see or hear but how I feel. From the moment he appeared I felt a love that seemed unfamiliar in my human experience but also familiar and remembered— one of those things that words don't convey at all well.

Because Emmanuel was so comfortable to me, trusting him was not difficult. What has been difficult is trusting all that has unfolded as a result of this meeting—private readings, workshops, lectures, world travel, this book— all beyond my conscious formulation or even ability, as I perceived myself. Nevertheless, the more I say 'yes' to what is offered, the more 'yes' becomes wisdom. To trust, to flow with it all is exquisite joy when I am able to allow it. The rewards are immediate and unmistakable. A feeling of deep peace and joy which in turn has helped me in my trusting. The result of this trust has been a positive upward spiralling in my life.

It has taken 12 years for me to know absolutely that Emmanuel will be there when I open to him. As he has explained, he does not leave the contact, I do. In order to live my life I have needed to juggle the two seemingly separated realities. Ultimately I know my task is to combine all things in the Now of Love. I am working to do that. My experiences with Emmanuel motivate me to evolve as a person until I can maintain that loving empathy with the world all the time.

Many people ask me who Emmanuel is. I still don't exactly know. Have we been together in past lifetimes? He says we have. Will we be together when I leave this physical body? "Absolutely," he promises. Is he part of my greater self? Perhaps, for we are all part of each other and of the greater Oneness. All I can say for certain is that I know a profound glory when I am connected to that light which, in turn, allows me to trust completely the sweetness of all that is. There are moments during our sessions when I am able to feel personally the all-encompassing love he brings. This is not merely vision or intellect but something far deeper and absolute.

It has also been a long road for me to travel to finally trust that I will not be exploited by either the world of spirit or by people. I had to learn to say 'no' when I am too tired, too distracted or personally too attached or detached to follow what would be the usual path of 'yes'. I have discovered my 'no' can also be part of the perfect plan.

Emmanuel has brought other treasures into my life: the wonderful people I meet, the mutual creation of this book, and the golden thread that has woven this enterprise together, my friend from eons past Judith Stanton. Never would I have met Ram Dass nor begun my workshop travels had it not been for her. Nor would I have had the insight or courage to begin this book at all. For this I am exceedingly grateful. But the greatest blessing she brings is to learn that God's angel can dress in blue jeans and sweat shirt, drive a van and excel in wry humor and madcap adventure and still fulfill the Plan of Salvation.

Thus every step along the way has brought teaching in wonderful ways. My task is to be open to allow what is to be received and utilized in my own growth. I have learned we hear with our hearts, not our ears. We understand with our intuition, not our minds.

So I offer you my dearest, wisest, sweetest, funniest, Absolute friend Emmanuel. I do this with more pride, love and gratitude than I could possibly express here. From this point on he speaks eloquently for himself.

Pat Rodegast

Emmanuel's
Book

1
An Overview
of the Human Adventure

The purpose of life is exploration.
Adventure. Learning. Pleasure.
And another step towards home.

Physical bodies
are rather like space suits.

Your physical bodies
can be symbols to you of restriction,
of ultimate pain and death,
of surprising and alarming needs
and of unexpected triviality
that knows no bounds of denigration.
Or they can be seen as chosen vehicles
that souls are inhabiting
because, rather like space suits,
they are necessary where you are.

*It is within your humanity
that you will learn
to recognize your divinity.*

The spiritual and the human have to walk hand in hand
otherwise the spiritual has no foundation
on which to take hold.

We are all one.
Ours is one reality, one energy, one perception.
The mind cannot grasp this fact
or accept it without battle
but the heart is yearning to know it.
Is this not life's purpose—
to know that you belong,
that you are safe and eternal,
to know that in your spirit reality
you are already one with God?

The human condition is not the antithesis of heaven.
It is the reproduction, within a limited vision,
manifest in physical form.
There is nothing in human experience
that does not exist in spirit.

This is why the human condition is a blessed one.
It is a mirror, a faithful replica
of the spirit's situation.

There is Divinity in all things
and in order to find that Divinity
one must work with the material at hand.
To disregard the clay
is to question the Divine Energy
that formed it.

Your text has been completed.

It is all here. There is nothing more
that humanity needs to hear in order to grow.
There will be no new teachings,
for they are unnecessary.
What we in spirit are here to do
is to point you
to what has already been given.

You live in a loving universe.
All of the forces are here to give you assistance,
to give you support.

We admire you tremendously.
Those of us who have been human
know full well the courage it takes.

*Life experiences are the outer symbol
of what the soul wants to know.*

Each soul enters into a physically symbolized reality
of that soul's conscious resistance to the inner Light.
So when you experience your human life,
view it as an outer manifestation of the longing
and also of the denial of that longing.
Every soul that incarnates carries with it negativity
or it would not take birth at all.

When you enter into a human life
you enter into a perceptual falsehood.
This is what the Eastern traditions call illusion.
If you treat the illusion as truth
you may become embittered, fearful and ill.

Instead, come into life assuming the perspective
of the creator of that life,
and see it all as a wondrous
and valuable learning experience.
*You can see within each circumstance
where you have been the potter of the clay
and in the outer reality of your creation
you can detect the mirror image
of your inner self.*

You are all on a path of self-responsiblity
from the moment you decide to reincarnate
until the time when the soul
decides it has had quite enough
and chooses to leave.

You are responsible
not only for your actions day to day
but for the very fact of your existence,
which extends your involvement
even beyond conception and the grave.

Each of you
is a portion of God
saying, "I will create."

It is quite impossible to recall
at what point in your existence
you, as part of God,
decided to become human.

Self-realization is God-realization.

Godliness cannot be superimposed on humanness.
It *is* humanness.
There is no separation.
Know yourself and you will know God.

Since your fundamental essence
is god energy,
which is creation,
you create.

You are the creator.
You are the creation.

You create your distortions
and you create your truths.
This is how you learn.

You chose the childhood environment
that was the most effective catalyst
to bring into focus those distortions
that you have selected to work on
in this lifetime.
It is a masterpiece of planning,
construction and tactic
that you have put into forming your body,
your mind and your emotions.
Trust the wisdom of your soul
that chose the infant circumstances
that formulated your concept of life.

You are the creator
of your planet
as well as your life.

This is a planet of choosing
where you can see both the darkness and light
and you have the freedom of choice.

Heightened awareness
is very much an integral part
of your planet's healing.

Your world is in physical crisis
but what is crisis?
A learning process.

Have faith in your fellow human beings.
They are educable.

In your total essence
you are already complete.

In the larger, all-encompassing reality,
all you dear souls who are in physical bodies
are still safely connected
to the Divine Laws of balance,
truth and unity.

Why are we here?

Because in the process of the soul's evolution
towards Oneness again
you have stopped at this level of consciousness
to remember who you are.
Why else would you have come into human form again
if not for this—
to remind the portions of you
that have forgotten their destination,
that have become lost and ensnared
in the outer expansion of their discovery,
that find themselves seemingly cut off
with no way to go Home?

Ask yourselves often in your lives,
"What have I forgotten?" When you are in pain,
"What is it that I don't remember?"
When you feel lost, "Where have I put
my real identity?"
It is a necessary step, my dears.
It is a great and glorious schoolroom.
And it is exactly where your consciousness belongs.
If it did not, you would not be here.

I am here to direct you Home.

This is a schoolroom of illusion.

Do not give permanent reality
to temporary things.

Once you have learned what you came to learn
the illusion can be left.
When you leave your text behind
see that it is in as excellent condition as possible
for the next class to use.
Knowing the purpose of that illusion
lends it respect.
It is all very tidy in the end.

As the desire to turn to the light increases
the soul knows where the resistance
still rests and takes the responsibility
for the exploration of that resistance.

Divine laws protect those of lesser awareness
from being given more choice, more responsibility
than they are able to handle.
The laws of likeness
place the human physically manifested reality
in a compatible level of consciousness.

One does not go from first grade into graduate
school, but by degrees.
As consciousness explores and creates itself
it moves slowly up the staircase of awareness.
It is not that one who is in deep darkness
and ignorance
suddenly plunges
into brilliant Light and total responsibility
as they lift from the physical body.
That would go against the Divine contract
of consciousness creating its own reality.

There are many levels of truth.
All of them contribute
to your total awareness.

Follow each thread in its own level of perception
and do not be confused by the lying together
of what seem to be opposite circumstances.
Ultimately, these dualities will be seen
as the necessary parts of the whole.

Yet it is in that very illusion
that the seed of your truth lies.
As you explore the pain in your life
and accept that pain as your own creation
you lead yourself directly to the illusion,
to the darkness within you.

Through understanding
and assuming full responsibility for that darkness,
you are then able
to unweave the tangle
of that particular area and bring it back
into the flow of life, into truth.

Your truth is your power.

The truth is the most freeing discovery you can make.

To be free of the fear of death,
to be free of distrust, of limitation,
to be free to be who you really are—
these are the gifts that you will receive
by paying the price of introspection and honesty.

Human life. is a most difficult classroom
until you learn the simple fact
that your truth is your power,
your salvation, your fulfillment,
your purpose and your way.
Once you can truly believe that
life becomes the joyous and abundant garden
that it is meant to be.

Joy is the sound
that echoes through the universe.

You hear that sound
when all of your struggles are seen
for the misapprehension that they are.
Then all of the confusions,
indeed, the human condition
at its best and at its worst
is seen as the illusory creation
of the soul's consciousness
seeking for the Oneness
that it already has.

Freedom is not an illusion.
Freedom is the natural way of being.
It is your birthright.
It is your home. ✿

Be willing to accept the shadows
that walk across the sun.

If this world were a perfect place
where would souls go to school?

Do not weep for the limitations
that you see existing in your world.
These limitations are there for a purpose.
Where would there be an opportunity to learn
if not in a world of imperfection?
Do not grieve for those who suffer,
who are subjected to limited capacities for living.

View your world as a transient place
where souls choose to come
because this is what they have selected
as their mode of learning
to the most minute detail. ✿

*All things are of God
and all consciousness
eventually knows
its oneness with God.*

The natural flow of consciousness
is towards Light.
The only resistance to Oneness
is within your own consciousness.
Here is the struggle.

As awareness expands, it cannot contract.
It can be distorted, but it cannot contract.
Once one has known a human consciousness
there would be little use
in being a blade of grass again,
for the karmic structure of the human being
is far more complex and aware.

Experiences manifested in your life
by the resistance you still possess
are there in the interest of truth and Light.
They show you the pain of these obstructions
so you will move through them.

In the faith of knowing that all things
are moving towards God
the obstructions take on
a different meaning and form.

They are there at the human level
to obstruct,
but at the ultimate level
to instruct.

Whether temporal or infinite,
all things are beautiful.

Some of you want to see
only what is already lighted,
hoping to avoid
what is still in darkness in your world.

Life does not have to be whitewashed
in order to be beautiful.

If you were to dissect a human being
and break him up into all his components
there would be no need to apologize
for any of the parts.

There is life in everything,
and there is consciousness in everything.

If the consciousness has reached the level
of a blade of grass
then that is where it is.
As the consciousness grows
and perceives itself in a more aware state
then it manifests in a more aware state.

The battle of light and darkness is within you.

This is not a world of victimization.
You are very much in control of your own life.
You are here to see where you are in Light
and also to find the residual areas of darkness
that are determined to sabotage that Light.

It is all too common
to feel victim to negativity
whereas the negativity
is really owned by the individual
as part of the karmic structure.

Darkness is a choice.

We are speaking of a denial of Light
not an absence of Light.
The concept of God being in all things, therefore,
is not so irreconcilable.

What is enlightenment?

Everything and nothing.
Let me see if I can find another way to put this.
If I say to you: "enlightenment is all-knowing,"
then I limit enlightenment.
If I say "enlightenment is all-loving,"
I limit love.
There can be no beginning and no end
and your human vocabulary is rife with limitation.

So let us say enlightenment
is being in the moment through eternity
without the intellect
but with the consciousness of all things.
It is absolute peace
without the awareness of non-peace.

It is absolute love
without the awareness of hate.

It is all things without end
having forgotten the illusion of ending.

It is bliss
without the memory of non-bliss

It is simply 'is-ness.'

It is you
without your physicality
without your personality
without your clothes on
without your obstructions
without your fears,
without your limitations and boundaries
without even the consciousness of self
except as the boundless perceiver
of infinite Light.

And that doesn't even describe it
but it is the best I can do at the moment.

*The layers upon layers of God denial
that encrust most souls in physical form
cannot be removed all at once
as in a surgical procedure.
They require
the gradual wearing away of resistance
through experience.*

Unfortunately, many experiences are painful
and negative until a certain point,
after which the learning can progress
through light and pleasure.
Where there is a deep desire to avoid
truth and responsibility, however,
pleasure can be used as escape
rather than learning.
Of course, there will be a denial
of responsibility for the pain,
but without the pain
the issue of responsibility would not be raised at all.

Be patient, then, and allow yourselves
to see the eroding of the layer upon layer of defense
that exists in the human cycles.
You will see that what is thought of as dire straits
is an opportunity to learn.

The ultimate oneness is mutuality,
not the erasure of self. ✿

The love that you hold for eternal truth
is the lifeline that leads you
through many incarnations
to the ultimate goal.

How delicate the thread and yet how strong!
Thus it is that the tapestry continues
and the weaving of each lifetime
brings you ever nearer to that longed-for time
when you can discontinue the reincarnational cycles
and follow your soul's desire
into higher levels of consciousness.

Ultimately, when all are again one with God
and are fully and consciously aware of it,
I promise you there will never be a moment
when you look back at a life and say,
"That was silly."
You will say,
"That was love seeking to know itself." ✿

*In spirit
the essence of your being
is love.*

I speak of the tenderness
and gentleness in your hearts
that are the very consciousness
of God.
That is your true identity.

When you touch a fellow human being in love
you are doing God's work.

See within each human being
a fallen angel.

There is an overall plan
of which you are not aware
and to which you can only contribute
by being who you are,
doing your best,
seeking your higher truth,
and following your heart.

This is God's plan of salvation—
not only of the soul consciousness
but of the earth itself.

The time is coming
when the culmination of eons of effort
will bring forth a renewed level of Light in your planet.
It will still be a schoolroom
that offers an opportunity to choose
between the negative and positive aspects.
There will, however, be more Light
and more awareness of this Light.
There will be a balance where love can flourish,
where kindness is a power and recognized as such,
where God can again be placed
in the center of consciousness of each human being.

The state of grace
needs the recipient
in order to be complete.

You are held in the hand of God
and totally loved
And when that love can be received
the circuit is completed.

When one moves closer to the source,
there is a moment
that is difficult to describe in any language.
The receiver becomes the giver
and the receptacle becomes the source.

. . .and then

the dance of eternity

really begins.

What do human beings look like to you, Emmanuel?

When I see a soul, I see Light—crystalline, pure, expanded and very beautiful. When I see a human being, I see that very same soul often cramped, struggling beneath an overlay of various diminishing hues that cause the brilliance to remain entrapped in the more opaque auric qualities. Beneath, of course, is the true Light of God in each soul. When I view you with my love, I see that Light very much as you do when you view each other with love.

Would you like to know the colors of doubt and fear? I will begin at the darkest color, which is denial of God, hate (the absence of love), and that is a very dark blackness. It is illusion, but a deep and dense illusion at times. Fear can be seen not only as the emotion itself, which is a closing down, a greyness, but also when connected to accompanying rage, it can be a scream of most intense and unpleasant sulphurish yellow.

Passion, in whatever manifestation, is various shades of red. Intellect is often yellow, and when it is being used for positive purposes, it is a golden, buttery yellow. When it is used to deny the heart, then it becomes a denser form of the same color.

Green is healing—the healing that is taking place within the body or the longing to heal others, which is often comingled with a soft pink which is love, human love.

Love of God glows white. Silver is communication, speaking. When it is speaking truth, it has brilliance and sparkle. When it is denying truth, or used manipulatively, it becomes steel grey.

Blue is a most radiant beam when it is connected to expanded spirituality, or to the empathetic relationship between human beings. There is also a deeper blue, every bit as clear and beautiful, as it reflects the deep emotions within yourselves when you are in direct and truthful communication with your own inner being.

Lavender, purple, these are the colors of spirit. Often, though not necessarily, spirit guides are seen to wear these colors when they first appear to you.

Gold is God's Love, given to the world through your willingness and your commitment to the works of such a calling.

You are all aware of these things. I speak to reawaken what each of you experienced in your very earliest days when you *saw* the colors surrounding the people in your life. They gave you distinct messages before you were able to understand words.

I see you all as rainbows.

2
God, Light, Christ, The Fall

You and God are one.

The ultimate blending together
of the mind, the heart, the soul and the body
will bring you into complete alignment.
This will then release you
from the reincarnational cycles.
Your ultimate self-realization
is the realization of God,
for you and God are one.
This is what you have travelled
these many, many lifetimes
to discover.

How can I know God or my deepest self when I'm not even sure I have any faith in the existence of these things?

Faith is not an intellectual thing.
It is a feeling.

You do not have to believe.
You only have to have the intent to believe.
You cannot will yourself to faith
but once you have removed the obstructions,
faith will be there
because it is a natural part of your being.

To truly know God, you must find out who you are.
For now, you can think of God as a higher truth,
a wider reality, natural order,
Divine safety and love.
By this I mean eternal reality
that is generous and kind and loving.
You can make any human image of this that you will
but once you have located your core,
your shining Light,
you will know who God is.

Your mind
cannot possibly understand God.
Your heart already knows.

Minds were designed for carrying out
the orders of the heart.
The mind answers the 'how,' not the 'what.'
The 'what' is a deeper matter.

The greatest war in life within each individual
is between the intellect and the heart—
where the heart is saying, "This is so"
and the intellect is saying,
"I don't understand, therefore I don't believe."

When you are with another human being
are you really communicating with the mind?
Or are you speaking to a soul
and the minds are scurrying around
trying to put it all into order and vocabulary?

When your mind asks "Why?"
you realize how easily it is satisfied
with a superficial answer.
When your heart asks "Why?"
it wants nothing but the truth of God.

The heart is an unerring compass
within each one of you.
The heart knows the soul
better than the mind does.
Unless your mind is in the service
of the heart
it becomes a warped and twisted master.

The only path that is right for you
is the one that is already designed within you.
To find this path
you have to hear your own heart.
There simply is no other way.

While the small mind, in its fear,
is rigid and controlling,
the deeper part of you will begin to whisper
the truth of your eternal safety
and your Oneness with God.
So listen to your heart.
This is where your Light is
and your truth.

Your will and God's will are the same.

This is such a sweet thing to tell you
and such a difficult thing to believe.
Once you begin to trust your heart
you will realize
that when something brings you joy and fulfillment
it is the will of God
speaking through your heart.

You were born
with the core of God within you.
Can you not trust
that this core speaks to you?
Trust too
that where your heart wishes to lead you
is also where God wishes to lead you.

Every time that yearning for God
manifests in your consciousness,
you smooth away a little more of the resistance,
the roughness, from the soul substance
that still, at some level, denies God's will.
If you count the grains of sand upon the shore
you will know how many times you have,
in this as well as past lifetimes,
yearned to realize your Oneness with God.

When you say from the heart,
"I choose to know God's will,"
then that is the fundamental use of free will.
It is only with freedom of choice
that this can take place.
In the act of surrender there can be no forcing.

Willing a release makes the release tighter
because it does not yield to will.
It yields to yielding.
Surrender to your own reality,
your own integrity.
All of these things can neither be taken away from you
nor fulfilled by anyone but you.
As the surrender deepens
the autonomy stands in bold relief.

By the act of surrender
you realize the absolute control
you have over your life.
Surrender is a choice—
an absolute, personal choice.

One cannot surrender completely
to anything but God.
All other surrender is symbolic.

Surrender can be proclaimed as the most selfish act
because it leads to total fulfillment.

When man's will is aligned with God's will
it is an effortless existence
in which the wisdom within you
is in a place of comfort
and loosely held control.

To know the presence of God's will
you need to listen to the many voices
that live in you.
You will find voices of fear,
rage, contradiction, obstinacy,
illusions of all sorts.
When those voices become familiar
then the gentleness, the softness,
warmth and Light of your inner wisdom
can the more easily be heard.
It contrasts with the cacophony
of those other voices
that are superimposed upon the inner knowing
that *is* God's will.

The final lesson for each soul
is the total surrender to the will of God
manifested in your own heart.

One does not have to stand against the gale.
One yields and becomes part of the wind.

The relationship of the individual soul
to the Universal Soul, to God,
is much the same as the oneness
of any energy factor to the source.

You are part
of that encircling and eternal force.
With each incarnation
you shed misunderstandings
that keep you separated from the Oneness.
It is only the confusion
that has divided you
and you are now finding your way back.

What is human 'divinity?'

Every cell of your body.
Every consciousness within you.
Every piece of humanness
and eons beyond.

Humankind
is a truly wondrous manifestation.
Do not be so critical when you deviate
from what your imagination tells you
must be the perfect state
before you allow yourself
to claim the God within.
Do you see how limiting that can be?

Each soul, as it becomes lighted,
is a power point.
How can you help light the world
if you do not let your light shine
though it be feeble at first?
Do not judge it by its kilowatt power.

Once the reality of your Divinity
is fully accepted,
you are free, you are free, you are free.

What is it like where you are, Emmanuel?

You know how it is
as you walk quietly through the woods.
You see a beautiful flower in its purity,
its innocence,
and its absolute trust of the laws of God.
You say to that flower,
"Oh, if only you could rule the world."
Well, here it does.

**How did you get to be a
God-realized being, Emmanuel?**

I have been through all of the human manifestations
that you are experiencing.
I, too, chose to leave the Oneness
to find my own consciousness
and bring back that consciousness
to add to the Light of God.
Along the way, I became forgetful,
as you have,
and I found myself wallowing, it seemed,
in a world so separate from God
that when the full realization of that horrifying belief
came to me,
I felt darkness all around.

Yet, as the longing and the pain increased,
I began to turn,
just as you have all done,
to seek the Light,
knowing that if I felt pain because of lack of Light
then there must *be* Light.
If darkness were my natural home
I would be comfortable there.

So I turned,
as you have done,
and climbed mountains and forded streams
and prayed in mosques and temples and churches
and followed teachers and stumbled and walked again
until I came to the time of evolution
when I could say truly and completely,
"I am one with God."
Then I was released from my reincarnational cycles.

**Why did we ever leave
the Oneness with God?**

The separation from God
began a journey of love.
The individuating consciousness seeks,
through the experience of human reality,
to know itself fully and completely
so that it can return to the Oneness
with a greater light and a greater understanding.
This adds to the reality of the Oneness
for all things are in a state of continual expansion
and creation.

God Supreme is everywhere
and yet without the experience of individuation,
the separation,
there would be an emptiness, a piece missing.
There would be the totality
without the consciousness to experience, to express,
and therefore to become a part
of that whirling universe
of eternal creation.

You are learning
to be creators in the deepest sense.
You are preparing
to join God in the act of creation.
The prodigal son returns.
In truth, one never 'fell' at all.
The Fall is a symbol of human experience.
As a symbol it is the forgetting
of the initial purpose of individuation,
getting lost in distraction,
the intent of the soul forgotten.
How could one leave God?
One *is* God.

Look to the reenactment of The Fall
as a wonderful map to take you to the Light.
You reexperience The Fall every lifetime.
Each incarnation
lets you discover where you still pull back, deny.
Your feelings of alienation
mirror the original separation,
the original forgetting.

Everything is in a state of pulsation:
the cosmic spheres, the galaxy, the earth,
the molecules that make up your body.
The separation and the return to God...
this is the creative pulsation of the universe.

The fall is the greatest act of love.

Who would leave the Oneness
if not to serve that Oneness through the leaving?
As you have roamed through centuries of unknowns,
always moving into the next moment of nothingness
to create Light,
you have fragmented from this journey
and have forgotten who you are
and why you have come.
And in the forgetting
you have taken on human personality
and gone to the particular
and in that particular
you find yourself now seemingly disconnected
from the Source,
reaching to return
through agonizing slowness,
back to the Oneness again.

How does one personalize being All-That-Is?
As you move *from* the Oneness
you move *with* the Oneness and you *are* the Oneness.
You are the Oneness expanding.
You are the Oneness in the act of creating.
For Creation must create
and thus there is no end
to this creating.

There is never a time
when Consciousness says,
"All right, I have done enough."
There is never a time
when Light says, "I have lighted enough,"
when Creation says, "I have created enough."
For when something *is*,
it simply must rest in its nature.
And the nature of Creation is to create.
The nature of Love is to love.

Therefore, you, as human personalities,
see yourselves separated from who you really are.
It is the clothes you have donned
in each incarnation
to impersonate who you are.
You can never identify yourself completely
with this impersonation,
for you know who you are
and that knowing always carries beyond
into the Greater Unknown and Home again
all at the same time.

That's quite a stretch.

It's only a stretch
if you believe in who you think you are
and that Home and the Great Unknown
are in different places.

Who was Jesus Christ?

Christ is a teacher.
I say 'is', not 'was'
for He still exists
and is very much available
to all of you here.
He is a Spirit of Love and Light,
of brotherhood and healing.
He is deeply involved
with the human world.

Jesus is my brother.
Your brother, as well.
A Being of Light.
There is not one person
who enters this physical world
who is not, at the core,
a Being of Light.

Jesus Christ
is the supreme example
of the reality of Light
in the human world.

Christ's birth
is the kiss of eternal love.
It is one of the greatest gifts
that God has given to humanity.
It is the symbol in human form
of the eternal reality of God,
His love, His nurturing,
and what has been termed His intervention.

The entire life of Christ,
if it could be reexperienced
in each one's consciousness,
would be the most magnificent symbology
of each soul's struggle—
a self-doubting, reaching, growing,
expanding, loving reality,
It would be the word of God
made physical.

Jesus' life was a mirror for humanity.
Even though there was God Consciousness
the soul of Jesus
as He experienced humanness
knew turmoil.
There was a great deal of identification
with the physical form
and therefore there were questions, fears, doubts.
But all that was given
in order to bring new and deeper understanding
into the human condition.
Jesus' struggle was a depiction
in which humanity could see its own reflection
and the infinite possibilities
of the growth process.
Most certainly a gift from God.

If Christ were a mirror for you
how would you see yourself?
How does this reflect each one of you?

Other prophets spoke in different modes
but Jesus spoke through the human experience.
Human experience was wedded to the spirit.
The lesson was lived and shown.
Christ was saying, "Look, humanity.
Look at what you can do.
See who you are."

Will Christ return
in form to earth someday?

I stand here to remind you
that within your own being
is the Christ that you seek.

As for the embodiment of that brilliant Light,
I think not.
Others can take that Light for themselves.
They then become teachers
in the name of and in the empowerment of
that central brilliance.
Remember that the spark
is lighted from the center
and that Light is available to everyone.

That blinding flash
exists in all of you.
As realization comes into human form,
it glows with its own Light
and this can be seen
as Christ Consciousness returned.

Heaven is the space within each one of you
that dances in the Light.

'Heaven' is a word that has been devised
to represent the unrepresentable.

Heaven is within your hearts,
within your consciousness,
and it is within your grasp
even as you walk at this moment.

Heaven is joy and love
and boundless enterprise
and limitless creativity.

Heaven is everything you are seeking
and more.

Heaven is your home.

3
Love

You will not exhaust
the love in the universe
if you were to absorb it
from now until the end of time.

Love is all that exists.

Love is the universal communication.
It is the energy that has created the
universe and is keeping it going.
God is love.
All matter is formed by love.
There is an organic love
that speaks to everyone
if they could but hear.
A leaf holds together
for love.

Love can turn the world around
and it does.
What did you think was spinning your planet
if it wasn't love
and what do you think the fires of your sun consist of
and the cells of your body
and the stars in your sky
and the consciousness in your heart?
It is all love.

There is nothing but love.
Don't let the masks and postures fool you.
Love is the glue
that holds the Universe together.
The greatest need in a soul
is to achieve that loving of self
which will bring about the unity
wherein the judgements
that have caused such pain
are eliminated.

True self-love is not ego.
True love is great humility.
Love and compassion for others
cannot exist
until there is a goodly supply for self.
How can you feel the love of God
if you do not love yourself?
Are they not one and the same thing?

Until you can accept yourself
you lock the doorway
to the expansion you all yearn for.
This expansion comes through your heart.
Be kind to yourselves.

Love requires no practice.
Love is.
One cannot practice is-ness.
One can, however,
practice the decision to love.

The path to love is found
by experiencing what it is like without love
just as the path to Light
is to be aware of darkness.
You make the supreme choice.
Love is not mastered.
It is allowed.

Love comes in many containers.
It can come through the flowing work of an artist.
It can be the magnificent self-sacrifice of a martyr.
It can be the firm resolution of a leader.
It can be the touch of a parent.
Something as simple
as taking the hand of a child crossing the street
is a monumental act of love.

Every act of kindness and love
adds more Light and more power
to God's Truth in your world.
To bring the concept of love
into your physical reality,
to live it as richly as you can,
is to answer the calling of the God within
that has decided to incarnate.

Everyone in your world is yearning
for that fulfillment.
This is not a substitute for God love,
but is a nourishing, energizing, freeing aspect
of the Universal Plan made physical.

There may be fear of dividing love
between God and one's mate.
I wish to say that there is no conflict.
The nurturing that you receive
on a physical level
is, in fact, beneficial
to your spiritual growth.
You yearn for love
as the flower yearns for the sun,
and you have as much right to it.

Does love survive death?

Love is eternal
It passes through every illusory barrier
such as time and space.
Love is an unbreakable connection.
Your consciousness weaves through the physical
to the non-physical and back again
even while you are all walking around
busily engaged in your daily tasks.

As you carry within you the love
and the yearning to return to God,
the sacrament of homecoming
is a constantly renewed reality within your life.
Your heart is returning you Home.

In your culture it is thought
that the mind must lead
and the heart must follow,
suspected of irrationality.
I wish to reverse that misconception
and to give you back your heart,
your soul energy, your spontaneity
and love of life.

The world does not have to be rational.
It has only to be experienced.
Rationality is the demand of the mind
that says to the heart,
"I will control here.
You are foolish and you know nothing."

Thought is a tool to take you to the gate.
Then you must leave your tools behind.

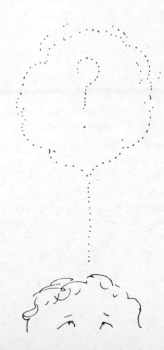

**How can we stop worrying
about the ones we love?**

By trusting
the absolute wisdom of each soul.
Worry is distrust
put into a slot
that seems socially acceptable.

If you say,
"I am worried about my children,"
everyone says, "Yes, of course,"
and thinks you are a good parent.
But if you should say,
"I really don't trust the Divine Plan,"
what do you think the reaction would be?

How do I open my heart
so I can hear God?

By relaxing all of the devices
that you have used through the centuries
to keep it closed.
The natural state of the heart is open.

Note how you struggle
against what you are seeking.
It will help you to answer
these questions.
How do I find my way?
How do I open my heart?
How do I touch the God within?
How do I hear the spirits that are with me?
How do I learn to love?
How do I grow to become who I am?
By ceasing to be who you are not.

There is not a heart that exists
in your human world
that, if it were assured of safety,
would not open instantly.
It is all an issue of fear.

4
The Path:
Task, Teachers, Practice

**If everyone in human form
chose life for their own growth,
then would you say
all of humanity
is on the spiritual path?**

Absolutely.

It's a beautiful thought, Emmanuel.

The entire universe
is a beautiful thought.

You will know
your next step
from this step.

You will never find it
any other way.
Your intellect
does not know it.
You cannot think
God's reality.
You can only
experience it.

You often misunderstand your path
as the ultimate symbol
rather than as a means.

Rather than go to the heart,
the inner sanctuary,
humankind builds symbols
of a reality that already exists.
It is a wonderful instinctual yearning
that gets misdirected,
in which the seeker
makes the seeking
the goal.

Rituals are not the path.
They are the reminder
that there is a path.

Whatever ritual speaks to you, hear it.
When it no longer speaks to you
seek another
if another is needed.

Let me offer you this practice.
See all things with love, as part of you.
Do you see how I have slipped in
the necessity to love yourself?
Some of you didn't even notice.

For example: a flower.
Touch it with your love,
not just visually, but experientially.
Breathe in its aroma; it is part of you.
See its beauty; that is who you are.
Touch its softness; that is your softness.
Feel the strength of its roots.
That is your strength, your rootedness in your world.
You would not see that flower
if it were not already a part of you.

Ultimately, your greatest teacher
is to live with an open heart.

Every moment of your life
is your task.
What do you do the best?
What gives you the greatest sense of fulfillment?
That is where your task lies.
Your own heart will lead the way
to your fulfillment
and to the part that you are here to play
in God's Plan of salvation.

There is no goal orientation
in God's Kingdom.
There is only Is-ness, Beingness.
There is nothing static about Is-ness.
It is a state of the most incredible creativity,
growth and movement.

Nothing in God's universe remains the same,
not even, I dare say,
the Consciousness of God Itself.
There is an eternity of learning.
Isn't that marvelous?

The most minute transformation
is like a pebble
dropped into a still lake.
The ripples spread out endlessly.

Is it necessary to have a teacher?

Do not overlook
the most important teacher that you have
which is your own intuitive knowing.

Teaching is always a reminder,
a stirring up of the embers.
This allows what is dormant in the consciousness
to come into active focus.
One cannot teach out of whole cloth.

You are all channels.
You are all open to hear your own hearts
or you would not be here.
From the deep well
of your own human experience
you bring up the cool clear waters
of love, of knowledge, of wisdom
to give to the rest
of your human community.
To the extent that you are in truth,
to that extent are you a light in the heavens
shining forth Love and Light and God.

But remember,
when a teacher ceases to learn
he ceases to teach.
Such a one becomes rigid and fixed—
a signpost, perhaps,
but not a teacher.

The concept of teacher as student
and student as teacher
is not new.
It has been spoken of by the wise souls
of every generation.
There is much learning
to be derived from the teaching process.
But the teacher must remain the student
if the teacher is to grow.

*Every religion at its roots
has been inspired by God
and then has been seized by the intellect
and limited, distorted and many times
all but destroyed.*

I do not speak against religion.
I question the use of dogma.
To believe in the God in everyone
is the ultimate religion.
It does not matter
what path you take to get there.

Religions should be respected
for the explosion of Light
that brought them into being.
A religion, however, must not be worshipped
as having more power than each individual
holds within himself or herself.
Although a religious tenet
may have been taught for centuries,
and perhaps because
it has been taught for centuries
and has refused to grow and bend
with the growing consciousness of humankind,
it needs to be held in question.
Always make your heart the final judge.

The God that exists within human beings
is alive and well.
Those who espouse a religious path
that by-passes the value of human experience
fear that in humanness there is no God.
Their vision of God
does not encompass the warmth,
compassion and vitality
that you who seek the God within
are able to experience.
Give your love and compassion
to those who deny their humanness.
Theirs is a painful path.

**Is self-sacrifice
a spiritual necessity?**

If you were a pitcher filled with water,
clear and beautiful,
you would be most happy to pour for others
as they came through your life.
But if you were an empty pitcher
what could you give to others
except a facsimile of giving,
which is no giving at all?
What you give then would have demand attached
because your own needs have not been met.

Nobility of purpose must be backed
by nobility of self.
Self-sacrifice has been lauded beyond its worth.
No one needs to sacrifice for others.
There is an illusion here that is very subtle.
When 'sacrifice' is painful
there may be an unwillingness to give at all.

When you are full
you give and it is joy.
It is love.

Meditation is a path
that will help you release
the treasures of self-love
that rest deep within you.

This may also, from time to time,
offer difficulties in that you will be forced
to see your imperfections.
These are transitory states.
They are areas where the life force
has been petrified.
When this force is freed
it will flow sweetly again, blissfully.
Listen to your inner being.
It is wiser than your conscious mind.

As meditation, almost anything will do:
music, a quiet walk, an excellent meal,
firelight, candlelight,
holding the hands of a loved one,
whatever causes you
to center into the joy of your beingness
and to disregard the clamoring
of your intellect.

Some of you tend to become too rigid in form.
There are as many ways to meditate
as there are people to walk the earth.
Everyone needs to go into their own inner silence,
their own inner truth,
in whatever way they can.
This inner illumination is your birthright.
It is the key to the essence of your being,
to your soul's wisdom.

In your meditative practice
see that time of quiet
as an open door.
Through that door
you walk into a broader light,
into a wider sense
of self and reality.
Definitions
are only for clarification,
not imprisonment.
Remember that.

When one comes to a threshold of expansion
in meditation,
there comes a time when the intellectual mind
is not capable of following.
To feel that you have somehow to keep control
through the intellect
puts a limitation on where this expansion
is trying to go.

As you ultimately move beyond
your intellectual mind
you will touch your soul mind.
The soul mind is able to give form and substance,
meaning and relationship
to the expanded consciousness
in meditation.

Let your prayer be an ongoing renewal.

You pray
by touching the deepest part of you
that longs, that needs, that Is.
Let it speak in its own language,
more often than not without words.

The longing itself
is the prayer of life,
"I want to be with you again, God.
I want to be Home."

There is no *how* to prayer.
It simply *is.*
It is a part of the Oneness.
It is a part of your coming Home.
Do it whatever way you like.

Prayer is to assure you
of your connection with Home,
much as when you were children
and you left for the day.
There was that moment of panic—
I'm sure you remember it—
when you had to call home
just to be sure
that it was still there.
Prayer is like that.
It is calling Home.

All levels of understanding and teaching
are available in your world.
It is where you yourselves
are able to hear
that you will feel an affinity.
When that affinity becomes less compelling
then you seek teachings of another form.

All true spiritual teachers
in any country and in any faith
have served the great purpose
of directing the human consciousness
individually and collectively
to the God within.

Leave your heart open to Divine guidance,
not passively as a leaf upon the river,
but as a navigator on that river
who may flow with the lovely depth
and swiftness of the current
yet who also takes responsibility
for his own craft.

You must go through your heart,
your love, your sense of self,
before you can touch
the expanded intuitive awareness.
You would, otherwise,
be in danger of losing your heart
in the seeking of intuition.
If you assume and develop
these powers
but have by-passed love,
then what do you have?

What can you lose
if you have your own heart?
And what can you win
if you do not?

**How long does it take
to reach enlightenment?**

All things in life
are dedicated to the purpose
of expanding awareness.
One never discards a portion of oneself.
One merely transforms it into Light
until the entire being is Light.

This is a minutely slow process.
You may feel as though
you are standing in the same place
as you were a month ago,
and yet you are not.
You have a month more
of life experience, and therefore
you are more aware
than you have ever been.

I say this to erase discouragement.
I do not say it to obliterate effort.
The more conscious the striving
the more rapid the growth. ❀

5
The Realms of Spirit

Breathe into your hearts
your deepest desire
to perceive Beings of Light
and put aside any expectations
of how we will be perceived.

You have no idea how limiting expectations can be.
Give yourselves permission,
at this very moment,
to touch the world of spirit.
All it takes is your permission.
We are here.
Sigh into it.
Your mind does not know the way.
Your heart has already been there.
And your soul has never left it.
Welcome home. 🍀

Am I here?
Yes, I am here.
Reach out your hand
and it will be touched.

If you say, "That's my imagination,"
so be it.
Then I am a figment of your imagination.
And so are you.
And so is your world.
And so is your longing.
And so is your love.
How can you do that to yourself?
How can you live in such pain?

Yes, I am here.
And so are you through eternity.

Do we exist?
Yes, we do.
And is there a God?
There is.
And are you frightened?
Yes. And are you confused?
Of course. And are you imperfect?
Absolutely. Perfectly imperfect,
and it's all right.
It's all part of the Plan.
It's all God's Love manifested
here and there and everywhere.

How can I best explain you
to acquaintances
locked in their rational minds,
even to my own rational mind?

I am aware I present a problem,
and do sincerely apologize.
I also smile a little, if you will forgive me.

Why is it so difficult to explain me?
Is it not because you yourself
are still a bit ashamed of your own longing,
of your own growing and blossoming beliefs?
Isn't it true that it is still uncomfortable
to say the word "God" in polite society?

I am no more or less a magic being than you.
I am spirit and you are spirit
I have a body and so do you.
Mine is slightly altered
by the altering of my consciousness.
You and I are both walking the same path.
We are seeking Truth and our souls
are yearning back toward the Oneness with God.
All of us are growing within our own realm.
There it is.

It is not such a big step between your reality and mine.
There is a belief that you who are in physical form
are the only solid existence in the universe.
This is clearly not true.
We all have our physical reality.
Mine may not be as photogenic as yours
but it certainly exists!

*There are as many spirits
involved in the human process
right at this moment
as there are human beings.*

There are many bridges being built.
Many doors are being opened
through which the light of unity
is streaming from the world of Greater Light
into your world of Becoming Light.

There are many beings of various intensities of Light,
physical yes, non-physical certainly,
all stirring around, intent on fulfilling
their own Selfhood.
The miracle of God's creation is evident
as one watches these darting sparks
of love and consciousness, weaving in and out,
lives upon lives touching and leaving,
loving and disappointing, but learning,
always learning.
It is a tapestry of such magnificence and marvel
that I cannot begin to tell you.

Do not despair. There is never a moment,
regardless of how it may seem,
when God is not fully aware
of every minute flicker of your human awareness.
It is only the shadows of your own self-forgetting
that cause the darkness to manifest.

Your world needs mine,
and mine, my dears, needs yours.
We must do this together.

As we meet more and more often,
threads of golden awareness
are weaving our realities together.
There will be, at some future time,
the most beautiful moment
when all the illusion is dispelled
and we stand in mutuality and in unity.

In the meantime,
it takes a great deal of faith to be human.
Does it not?

**Does every person
have a guide?**

Not a soul exists
without at least one accompanying spirit.

You are guided.
I wish to reaffirm that for you.
Some of us who no longer need to be human
exist in our realm of consciousness
to guide and to teach.
Meet us as friends.
Allow us into your lives.
We do not wish to be worshipped.
Worship belongs to One only.
That is God.
We are here to be heard and to be spoken to
just as you are.
There are many of us who are called to this serving,
to this joy of reaching you who are seeking us.
We are the bridge between the human yearning
and the spirit truth.
This is our chosen task.

We can guide you to deeper understanding.
We can assure you that you go on forever,
that you are eternally loved and tended.
This is all we can do.
Beyond that, you must walk it step by step.

You are here to live your life.
My function, through my love,
is to shine the Light on the areas
that will direct you towards your own inner Light.

Who are our guides?
How can we reach them?

Your guides are spirits on the plane of forgiveness
who have ultimately forgiven themselves.
They now seek to aid you
in your own self-forgiveness
and in finding the true Christ
within each one of you.

How can you find them?
Through meditation, through prayer,
through opening your heart
to the worthiness to receive such guidance,
by being willing
to hear what you do not expect to hear or,
perhaps, what you do not want to hear.

Be open to receive. It comes slowly, you know.
This illusory wall between my reality and yours
has a seemingly solid dimension on your side.
I see it not at all.

Since you regard it as a reality,
it becomes one.

Begin to allow for the disintegration of this creation
that separates our worlds.
Be willing to puncture holes in it from time to time,
and to see the Light coming through.

The responsibility for asking for the teaching
must be yours.
The responsibility for utilizing the teaching
must be yours.
We in spirit cannot shout at you
through the doorways of resistance.
We subtly speak to you in sleep.
in meditation, in inspiration,
until you are ready and willing
to open to a clearer means of communication.
You receive these communications not only audibly
but in your hearts as well.
The doors are open.
The teachers are ready.

Can we trust
the guidance
we receive?

You must test it. You must check it.
You must hear what is being told
and ultimately allow your heart
and your own inner wisdom,
your own intuition, to be the final authority.
Accept nothing that does not sound right to you.
This responsibility must never be abdicated.
Remember, you are God, my dears.
Trust that part of you.

There are seraphims
who touch down upon the earth
when there is great need.
Such beings do not have to exist
through an entire lifetime.
One will suddenly appear
and then simply not be there any longer
and you will say to each other,
"Do you remember that remarkable man?"
"Wasn't he extraordinary?"
"I wonder what her name is."
"I wonder where she lives."

**Are souls that are not guides
able to communicate?**

Of course.
The connection of love is never broken.

The golden chain of love is eternal
and when there is genuine need
the soul is called wherever it may be.
Even if the soul has reincarnated,
the soul will come.
This is something important to know.

There is mercy, balance
and love in the universe.

On dark forces:

One is not invaded by darkness.
One has courted that darkness.
It is a matter of addressing the host
rather than chastising the guests.
Compassion, rather than punishment, is in order
for those souls beginning to seek.
You would not walk into a kindergarten
and denounce the children as lost souls
because they cannot read and write.

The darkness needs to be seen,
not as a threat,
but as an opportunity
to love.

You have no idea
how often the exchange
between your world
and mine takes place.
It is a constant thing.
The separation of our worlds
is a thin screen of learned illusion.

When you enter into the womb
you begin to acclimate to a limited reality.
There is, at that moment of birth,
not an instantaneous confinement in the body
but simply an awareness
that you have entered upon a journey,
that it is important, and there are many things to learn.
Your total consciousness
does not *fit* into that small body.
Somewhere you hear a baby crying and you know
that it's you.
Identification with that "you-ness"
takes many months, indeed years, to accomplish.

6
Duality:
Evil, Darkness, Pain

You are like children in a lighted room
who close their eyes
and say
they are afraid of the dark.

All darkness
is a disturbance of light.

What is evil but forgetfulness?

You need know
the nature of darkness.
It is finite. ✿

Some of you perhaps are wondering
why I always promise goodness,
why I don't say anything about darkness.
Simply because, from my perspective,
it does not exist.

I see you all individually as Beings of Light
working through the maze
of your own misconceptions.
You are learning. You are learning. You are learning.
You are finding out who you are.
You are altering the beliefs
that brought you into your physical world:
the belief in darkness,
the belief in the power of fear,
the belief that anger has a force
that can stand against love.

All these things are here for you to learn
but it is you who have brought them.
In your belief in such things
you have created them.
You have not created them in order to be defeated
but to learn.
Of course there seems to be darkness in all of you,
however it is not as you believe it to be.
It is only a shadow, cast by the interference
of your false illusions,
that cuts you off from the Light.

I will continue to instruct
in the language of Light and Love
for this is the only language I know.

Nothing exists in the human world that is not Godly.

It is God's world.
Around the distortion and the duality of your earth
is the Oneness of God's Love.
There is an undivided reality
that embraces your dualistic world
that is truly governed
by Love and Light and Truth.

*Evil is only ignorance
of Divine Will and Divine Law.*
None would resist God's Will
if they were aware
that it consists of their own joy,
bliss and eternal happiness.

Although the negative energies
may seem not to flow with God's natural Laws,
they are indeed present in your physical world
doing God's Work.
Without them, you would not be offered
a choice between darkness and Light
and your growth process would be much hindered.
So, you see, they are a necessary ingredient.
These energies are not masters, they are servants
of God's Will,
although they would be the last to admit that.

Although the dualism of mankind may seem so erratic,
always encircling and protecting
is the Universal Wisdom.
This state of Grace that surrounds you
is a loving and eternal Light
that allows within it the growth process.

Negativity has within it
the seeds of its own destruction. ❀

You experience as you believe.
The very world in which you exist,
the positive and negative alike,
is a product of what you hold to be true.

There is within each one of you
the kernel that has contributed
to the circumstances of this moment
in your particular area of the country,
in your particular time of the evolutionary process. ❀

In your dualistic world
there is great joy in dichotomy.
It is part of the game of life you sometimes engage in
that delights in pitting one side against the other
in order to find a universal truth.
This duality can, perhaps,
serve the purpose of ultimate unification
but only if you know that that is the intent.
Those who are great thinkers
have enjoyed for centuries separating the truth
in order to dissect it. Then they forget
the whole cloth they took it from,
and that creates pain and confusion.

As long as there are those who are seeking Light
there will be people who have shadows
that seem to follow them.
When the image can be altered
so that they can see that the shadow is only
their own blocking of the Light,
then there will be no fear, no illusion,
and only the joy of leaving a physical body
when one is quite through with it.

The duality of your earth
has a Divine purpose.

You have participated in its creation in that form
because that is where your personal reality is now.

Though you may live in it,
you are not trapped in it.
It is not your prison
but your schoolroom.
You are using duality to help you find unity
not to be lost in the duality.

There are, in fact, no direct opposites.
They only seem so
in that one is speaking of Divine Law
perceived from different areas of understanding.

I find it hard to accept
the pain of the lower echelon
of the food chain.

And therein lies the struggle
for those who are caught
in thinking so much about their fate.
However in the consciousness
of those smaller animals
there is no past and no future,
no shoulds and no shouldn'ts.
There simply *is*.
This release from judgement allows
for total acceptance of the circumstances.

But a baby bird
falling out of its nest...
what can help that bird?

Love.

And if a cat comes over
and kills the bird...
then what can help the bird?

Love. Not only for the bird
but also for the cat.

When you see, in what is labelled the predator,
cruelty, anger, unfeelingness,
you are merely seeing a reflection.
When, in the motions of two consciousnesses
coming together to fulfill a mutual contract,
you can see, behind the act,
the love, the balance, the reason, the purpose,
you will no longer feel yourself burdened
by that illusion that causes you to cringe.

As you accept—not blindly, not uncaringly,
but with an ever-deepening awareness—
those circumstances involved in human existence,
you will more and more
be reflecting your own Light.
There will come a day
when regardless of what is transpiring
in the human community, you will regard it
as a blaze of Light,
and you will be free.

Is it possible that the bird
would fall out of its nest
as a gift to the cat?

And as a gift to itself.
God, in His Consciousness, I dare say,
would see the fall
and ultimate demise of that bird
as a time of joyous reunion,
as Light coming Home.

If you were to climb the highest mountain
and look at your world,
you would see
much more Light than darkness,
much more love than hate,
much more kindness than violence.
It is only that these negative areas
are more vocal.
They are calling for help.
They are like small children, lost and fearful.
Knowing not what else to do,
they shout and scream and strike out.

Pray for them.
Pray for all of them
and do not fear.

**Can we experience
ecstasy on this plane
without corresponding depression?**

Only when you can view
depression and ecstasy as one.

It requires an initial leap of faith
to see another reality
in the experience of pain.
Pain and darkness
are extremely compelling.

You have physical bodies that ache
and sometimes scream.
You have emotions that seem to tear you apart.
I urge you in those times of such stress,
ask yourselves who it is that is experiencing this.
And the 'who' that is aware of the experiencing,
not lost in it, but aware of it,
will be the bearer of the Light.

In your concept of the cosmos,
be aware of the stability
that allows for individual chaos.

The way to transform violence
back into the beautiful Light force
that it truly is
is the exquisite task of seeing violence,
not as it presents itself, but as the force
that it will ultimately become.
There is a key here for all of you:
see even in the most despicable
the Divine quality that has become distorted.

What would violence be in its Divine state
before it has been twisted into vicious aggression?
It is the power to stand
and to speak and to witness
to a deep faith in the Light.

Violence is a form of witnessing to,
but it is witnessing to distortion
rather than to truth.
There is courage in violence.
Don't forget that for one moment.
It is stepping out,
going beyond the 'shoulds' and 'shouldn'ts.'
It is saying, "I exist and I must be seen."
Hear that in the context of spiritual teaching
and you will find the means by which violence
can be transformed within yourself
and therefore within the world.

Murder, violence, cruelty,
viciousness, wickedness—yes, this all exists,
just as kindergarten exists before first grade.
Violence is painful for you who look
from a level beyond (not better than
but certainly wiser than), and see with anguish
the anguish that creates the anguish.

Do not be afraid of terror.
Do not react violently to violence.
Do not feel pain about pain.
By doing so, you perpetuate
what you are seeking to avoid.
When you pass judgement on such things
you are limiting God's reality
to your human understanding.

From where you sit, there is right and wrong
and from where I sit, there is truth.
Many in your human world might relish
what punishment may come to the murderer
as he enters into another life
to atone for his violence.
Yet you cannot judge that.
You can only bless and pray
and open and trust.

**If we finally all
become one soul again,
then do I
have to become part of the whole
with Hitler?**

My dear, when you and Hitler
are ready to become one,
all of the animosity
will have been altered
to Light and Truth.

*Your world is a place
of the bending of the Light.*

But the Light must be there
or you have no world at all.

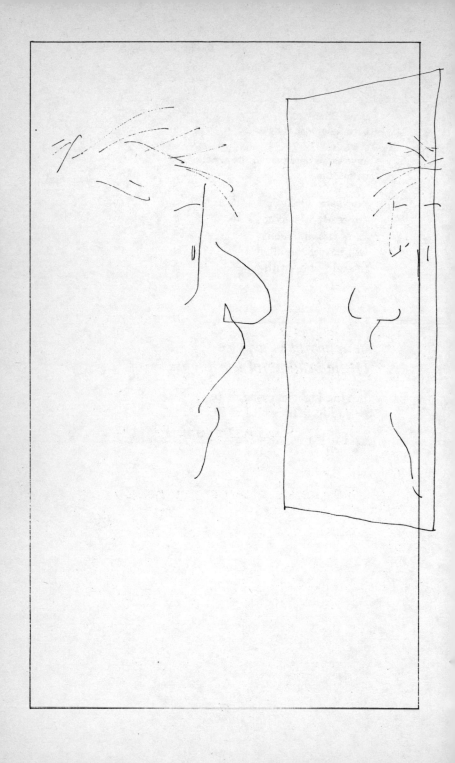

7
Meeting Imperfection: Fear, Doubt, and Other Stumbling Blocks

What you are is perfect imperfection

Your less evolved areas have a right to be.
They whisper of things past.
They whisper of confusion, of unfulfillment
and of the pain of the soul separated from its God
and the longing for that Oneness again.

Realize that on this earth
there can be only relative perfection.
Realize too that you do not need to be perfect
to be loved. Love each other in your imperfections,
tenderly and completely. Be gentle with yourselves.
The demand for perfection on the physical plane
can be your worst enemy.

To insist on perfection precludes growth.
To accept imperfection as part of your humanness
is to grow.
If you can love the part of you that you think
is imperfect
then the act of transformation can begin.
When you judge it and throw it out of your heart
it becomes a hardened shell that blocks the Light.

If you deny what is your nature
you become deeply attached to that denial.
When you accept what is there, in its truth,
then you are released.
One does not release through rejection.
One releases through love.

To strive for Light is a beautiful calling
but you cannot find the Light
until you acknowledge the darkness.
Souls who strive in perfect yearning
are as close to perfection
as anyone in human form can be.
Who you are is a necessary step
to being who you will be, and so it goes
through eternity.

Be comfortable but not complacent
with your imperfections.

Who demands perfection?
Only you souls who are locked in human form
believe somehow that perfection is the requirement.
It is not. The requirement is sincerity,
an open heart.
That is the perfection that is demanded—
the perfect longing.

The perfection of the universe
is an encompassing reality
around the imperfection
of your human world.

Look to understand your negative feelings
as a loving mother would understand
a confused and frightened child.

When the denial of God within you
is being challenged
it is a most propitious time of your life.
Do not deny the part of you that is in darkness
or it will manifest again.

When you become aware of misjudgement,
of ill-timed, ill-conceived thought and action,
when you recognize your desire for vengeance,
your anger or unforgivingness,
that is the time for self-congratulation.
Your new insight now allows you to handle these things
in a far more conscious way.
It is an opportunity.
A door has been opened.
A light has been turned on.

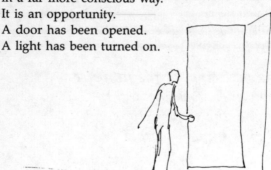

With awareness, you give yourself the gift
of an opening for growth and change.
Do not criticize yourself
because in darkness you could not see.

When you find the Light within you
you will know that you have always
been in the center of wisdom.
As you probe deeper into who you really are,
with your lightedness and your confusion,
with your angers, longings and distortions,
you will find the true living God.
Then you will say:
"I have known you all my life
and I have called you by many different names.
I have called you mother and father and child.
I have called you lover.
I have called you sun and flowers.
I have called you my heart.
But I never, until this moment,
called you Myself."

How can I forgive myself?

How can you not forgive yourself
for being exactly who you are?

To find the God within you
you must go through the portal of self-acceptance
as you are now.
Yes, all your faults and imperfections,
all your little secret, fearful uglinesses
that you are loathe to admit to yourself
are already known.
They are part of the Divine Plan.

True acceptance is saying, "It's all right,
it's all right, it's all right."

Self-acceptance
by-passes the need for self-forgiveness.

**How do I meet something
I'm ashamed of
or sorry for?**

With honest remorse.
Honest remorse springs from the heart
and quickly cleanses.

Responsibility for an act is commendable.
Responsibility and guilt are two different things.
Guilt is negative, unrealistic.
Responsibility is mature and will take you
out of the forest and into the Light.

In the feeling that your imperfection
is liable for another's pain,
you pave your world with guilt.

The most destructive, the most useless,
the most stagnant energy of all is guilt.
It means nothing and glues all things to a stop.
There is a sense of blindness, of suffocation
and aloneness. The world is opaque.
There is seemingly no escape.

It is the denial of the God Light within you
and of the yearning to be at one with God
that causes the very real sense of guilt.
That is the self-betrayal of the soul.

Not only is there no punishment in God,
but there is no punishment in the universe.
You dear human beings seem to feel
that punishment had better be self-inflicted
before God gets to you.

How do I conquer pride?

You don't conquer it.
Pride is not your enemy.
It is only part of your illusion.

Those who feel pride
have already felt the blow of humiliation.

Accept your pride as a child's need
and go behind it into the pain
that erected the wall of pride.
You will find
a most beautiful blossoming consciousness
that, in order to survive,
put on the armor of pride.

Specialness is something that separates you.

Uniqueness is something that blends you
together with your fellow human beings and yet
it allows you to contribute what no one else can.

Go through the unlayering of this human experience
and you will fall in love with yourself.

Vanity is the need to establish
a pleasant connection with the self.
Be patient and gentle with it.
Once you have learned to admire yourself
which, indeed, is absolutely deserved,
then you will go deeper
for you will have found
at least the shell of security.

Let me remind you that beneath the vanity
may lie a trap
and you know this one very well.
I point it out to you
so that you can become free of it.
Once you have loved yourself on the surface
and have felt vain in that regard,
there develops the gnawing doubt
that you are never seen for who you really are,
that you are only seen for the mask
that you have learned to present.

Once you find that your vanity has become a trap
you will begin to let it go
for it no longer serves your purpose.
But never doubt the value of it.
It is only a misrepresentation
of what you are truly seeking.
But then
if you will stand and look around you
in your world, isn't everything?

Please talk about anger.
It is such a spiritual downer.
What are some practical ways
to deal with it?

Stop calling it a spiritual downer, for one.
The fact that you can spontaneously feel anything
is a joy and a remarkable gift.
Are you aware of how many human beings believe
they must filter even the most intense emotions
through the intellect in order to maintain control?
A most painful circumstance.

Celebrate your spontaneity.
It is not a spiritual downer
but an indication that if your anger can erupt
so can your heart open
and so can God speak to you.

Anger
is a protective device.

It is quite enough
for you to experience your anger.

Nothing more need be done with it.

Underneath anger
is always fear
and underneath fear
is always
longing.

Fear
is one of the major cornerstones
of the karmic condition.
It speaks
to the distrust of eternal love.

It is a disbelief
in yourself.
It is an extreme perversion
of truth and light
and love,
which is precisely what your world
is all about—
the healing
of the extreme distortions
of truth and light
and love.

Fear is a fungus
that grows rapidly in the dark places
of the consciousness.
It is the most powerful of doors
that closes off the Word
and the Light of God.

Fear
is the dragon at the gate.
It is denial of Light
and denial of Light
is resistance to God.
It is the falsehood that separates you
from God.

What are we really afraid of?

You fear humiliation.

You fear to be wrong.

You fear
that if your knowing
is brought into your human experience
it will dissolve.

You fear to trust truth.

You fear to love in an imperfect world.

You can allay fear
through prayer, through meditation,
through clear thinking.
Try to accept
your areas of ignorance and reluctance
as the parent accepts the unreasonableness
of the child.
Understand
what this darkness is saying.
By accepting that erroneous thought process
into your own being
you bring it under your roof
and are able to alter it to the Light.

Listen to your fear
with a wise ear.
What are you afraid of in life?
What are you afraid of in yourself?
You must challenge fear
and ask it what it means to say.

As you go into the fear
with eyes open, heart open
and courage flowing freely,
you will see
that fear is only an empty room.
Fear is only as strong as your avoidance of it.
The greater your reluctance
to see the fear,
to accept it and embrace it,
the more power you allow it.

Fear is the unknown.
It is the imagination.
It is not reality.

There is nothing to fear in the universe.
Even death,
which is a fundamental truth and a necessity
in your particular scale of development,
has nothing to fear in it.

Rest yourself
in the reality of God's eternal
and everlasting Presence
and know
that there are plans deeper,
there is consciousness wiser,
loving hearts far more powerful,
than any that walk your earth.
I bless you
with the awareness
of your eternal safety.

It is not a matter of destroying fear
but of knowing its nature
and of seeing it as a less powerful force
than the power of love.

Fear is a trick, a sham,
a sleight of hand.
It is illusion.
The master magicians are heavily at work
in your world.
Demand to see up the sleeve,
behind the back
and underneath the table.
Expose the magician for what he is.
The magician of fear is a humbug.

Fear
is only looking in the mirror
and making faces
at oneself. ✤

Fear of the unknown
is forgetfulness.
There is no such thing
as the "unknown"
to the soul.
There is a natural fear
and resistance
when one does not recall
one's own Divinity.

You are safe. You are safe.
You are infinitely safe.
Oh, my dears,
if I could only make it possible
for you to experience the loving, gentle kindness
of the universe,
the balance, the fairness,
the sweetness and the joy.
there would never be another moment of fear
in your entire lives.
And this is true. ✤

*The serpent
in the Garden of Eden
is not sexuality.
It is doubt.* ❀

Do you doubt
that you are here as a spirit being
to function within a physical reality?
Of course you do.
Let me assure you that this
is a common misconception.

There is, all too often,
a feeling of non-worth,
of limitation,
at times of hopelessness and futility,
because of the constrictions of the physical body.
Yet within the structure
of your physical realm
great progress can be made.
This is the purpose of reincarnation. ❀

As long as there is a material body
you are carrying doubt.
Do not despise your doubting.
That is the human condition.
When there is no more doubt
you do not need to be human.

Know that your every step is unerringly guided
on a perfect route to your destination.
Whatever you may consider to be a side road
is not a side road at all
but the best of all possible paths.
It is only by going into the caverns of doubt
that you find the truth and the Light.

At times of giant steps
in the soul's evolutionary expansion
there are moments of great insecurity.
Let me offer you an analogy.
When you take your foot from one rung of a ladder
to put it on the next,
there is nothing for your foot to stand on
for that brief moment.
If you were to focus all of your attention
and identify all of your reality
with the sole of that suspended foot,
you would truly be in a state of terror.
You do not see
the hands holding the sides of the ladder
or the other foot that is firmly planted
on the rung beneath.

**Would you speak about
ridding oneself of attachment?**

It depends on what you feel attached to.
There is nothing wrong with attachment
if it does not limit you.

Attachment, in the negative sense,
is aligning yourself
with a physically materialized reality
and saying,
"This is where I'm safe,
this is where I have power
and this is where I'm going to stay."

But physical things can be beautiful.
And there is joy in beauty.
It is not the material object that is the joy;
it is your appreciation of it
and whatever can teach you joy and pleasure
has value.

If detachment were the order of the day
then oneness would be eliminated
from your physical schoolroom.
How would Oneness then be learned?
One needs to practice with that sort of thing.
How would you begin to understand
where you yourself avoid
or interfere
with the very Oneness
you are seeking to learn?
Without the reaching,
the longing,
the need for each other,
there would be no human community.

One of the fondest dreams that we in spirit hold
is of that moment
when all souls, all hearts, all hands,
will reach out to touch each other.
There will be no detachment then,
only a glorious Light.

Just to add a note of encouragement,
this is beginning to happen.

**How do we experience
painful circumstances
without becoming
embittered by them?**

By seeing them as lessons
and not as retribution.

*Trust life, my friends.
However far afield
life seems to take you,
this trip is necessary.*

You have come
to traverse a wide terrain of experience
in order to verify where truth lies
and where your distortion is in that terrain.
You will then be able
to return to your home center,
your soul self,
refreshed and wiser.

Whatever satellite goals may be found in life
the singular intent is always
the soul's process
of becoming one with Self and God.

Be comforted
and walk your life in Light and trust
for nothing will come to you
that is not meant to be.
There is nothing that can happen in your life
that in any way threatens your soul.
Indeed, all of life experience
enhances its awareness.
There is nothing that does not serve
the process of your soul's growth.

Until there is a fundamental trust
there will always be that sense
that something is left undone,
that something is waiting in the wings
to charge out
during a moment of joyous fulfillment
to shout,
"Aha! You forgot about this one.
You're not perfect after all."
And the sky will come tumbling down.

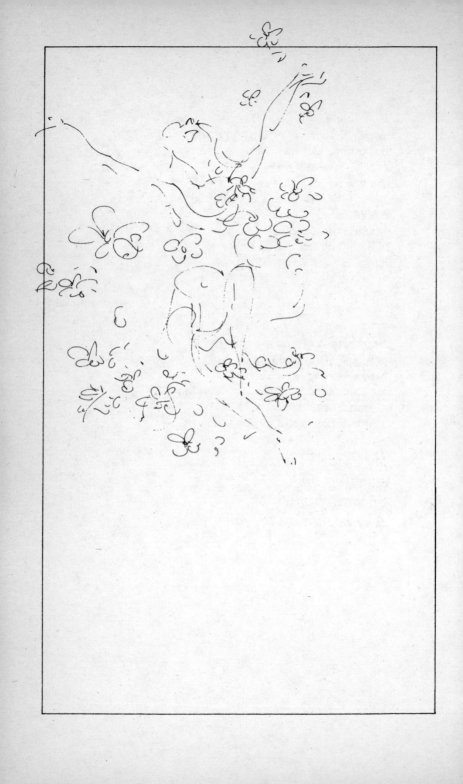

8
The Feast of Life:
Creation, Joy,
Abundance, Fulfillment

Joy is the God within you
standing up.
Shaking himself off.
And beginning to smile. ❀

In your joy
you are celebrating God.
You are celebrating the feast of life.

This is not something to be denigrated
on the grounds that there is more to life
than pleasure.
Certainly there is more.
There is an infinity of more.
One is never finished
with the process of growth,
of seeking, serving, loving.
The delights of the physical world
are the delights of the spirit world.
It is all one.
Your human joy will not take you away
from your love for God.
Love is love.
If you cannot tolerate human bliss
how will you withstand the bliss
of eternal Oneness?

If you were to check into the consciousness
of a rock
you would find a great deal of pleasure there.
You would find
a sense of Oneness that is comforting,
a delight in being a rock.
In the flow of its being
a rock is in a state of ecstasy.

Ecstasy cannot be scaled
on a rating from one to ten.
It is ecstasy.

Why are you all so suspicious of joy and softness?
Is this not also God's world?
Joy is a natural ingredient of life.

You human beings tend to be hurried and pressured
and thereby deny yourselves the exquisite pleasure
of savoring your lives.
In this way, a great amount of joy
and sweetness goes unnoticed.
If life is lived with care and attention
it will give you the sustenance
and richness you long for.
Allow yourselves to renew your commitment
to your lives and to yourselves
many times a day.

You feel that because you yearn for the warmth
and the softness of life
that this will somehow lull you into inactivity?
Must there always be a harsh outer reality
to remind you of God?
If you cannot trust beauty where you find it
how can you open your heart
to Oneness with God
which is eternal beauty?

Would it not be more suited
to the inner longing of each soul
to envision eternal Consciousness
as a gentle laugh
rather than a serious contemplation?

Life is only ponderous
when you are not connected to everlasting joy.
A great deal of solemnity serves no function.
You need to laugh.
You need to play, each in his own way.

Childlike qualities are Godlike qualities
in their spontaneity and joy.
Even the foolishness and the fun,
the dancing, the love,
the surrender, the abandon,
the lightness are part of the growing
pulsating human being
that is a blessing to your world.

God did not design pain and suffering.
Resistance designed pain and suffering.
God's Will is to light the world
with peace, joy, health and abundance.
And with the awareness
that this is a temporary stopover.

Joy is learning.
Joy is experiencing without pain.

Once you have accepted without question
that you exist in eternity as a conscious being,
that we in spirit exist, that God exists,
then the outer circumstances of your life
will lighten perceptibly.
You will not create or call to you
any darkness or distortion.
It does not mean that there will be one section
of your geographical earth called "Eden,"
but it means that you will have an awareness
of the true meaning of events.

As long as you inhabit the physical body
you will be subject to the physical world
yet the experience will be totally different.
There will be no pain.
This is not compromise. It is not saying,
"Well, then, I understand I am eternal
and so this agony doesn't mean anything,"
No. No. You will experience no agony,
literally as well as figuratively and conceptually.
This is not rationalization.
That would be a trap.
It is total absorption in the truth.

Because you see pain and joy
through the telescope of past human teachings,
you find it difficult to believe that you can exist
in a state of joy where pain can be dissolved
into the reality of joy without denial.
Joy simply alters pain's existence.

You need to know the great power that lies
in the act of visualization.

Vision is spiritual reality, and all things
that exist in your world first existed in spirit.
The concept comes first, then the physical,
which is denser matter, follows.

Once you challenge your preconceptions,
they become misconceptions.
The diameters of your awareness expand.
A wall, for instance, is no longer only a wall
but a bit of moving, vibrating consciousness.

Anything that can be envisioned
can be brought into your physical reality.

Whenever the feeling comes over you
that you have no choices
I urge you to call a halt to everything.
This is a trick you play on yourself
to avoid having to assume
the responsibility and therefore the joy
of life.

Envision, instead, what it is you truly want.
Test it. Be careful of this, my friends,
because if you envision something quite casually
and do it with conviction,
even though you may not be sure you want it,
it will manifest.
This is neither magic nor false hope.
It is the reality of the power
of your creative impulse.
This is why it is so important to develop
self-awareness to the depths of your ability
so that no creation can come about in your life
without your having made the choice.

You have designed your life yourself.
You have created nothing in your outer reality
that is stranger to you.
The inestimable joy of human manifestation
is to see around you
in what seem to be outer circumstances
what you truly believe as a soul.

Look at your physical manifestation as a symbol
and view your body as an extension of your soul,
the spoken word of your being.

Your life is not your master.
It is your child. ✿

Your joy of creation
must not be limited
to humankind.

There is, for instance, a great deal of enjoyment
in consciousness creating a portion of itself
in the form of other beings that exist in your world.
What delight you would experience in creating
from your own consciousness, a beautiful flower!
What pleasure, too, a sleek cat
or a monstrous elephant!
I am not being fanciful here.
I am explaining the way consciousness
creates its own self for exploration.
So where, in the consciousness of the universe,
there is the proclivity
to experience oneself as a flower
then a flower evolves.

Since you are in human form
it is understandably difficult to think of yourself
as having consciousness beyond your humanness
and still choosing to create a portion of yourself
as a "lesser" being. So I will put that aside
and let your imagination play.

You can create for yourself
a garden of bliss
if you believe in it.
And you can create for yourself
intolerable suffering
if you believe
that it is necessary.

This is not intellectual.
None of you wants to suffer.
But there are belief systems
that are handed down
from generation to generation
that perpetuate these beliefs.
It would be interesting for you
to speak to the oldest member
of your family and ask them
about the family superstitions,
the beliefs.
What is the structure
within which you have lived your life?
It will be illuminating.

**Is working for material things
a hindrance
to our spiritual purpose?**

Not if you see material things
as materialized consciousness.
When one is in the material world
one must have food and clothing.
And one desires a home that is beautiful,
comfortable, a place to be.

These are the accoutrements of self-love.
When self-love is truly acknowledged
you will not deny yourself any of these things.
Self-love will open your hands
to receive as well as to give.
And certainly it is not taking something away
from someone else.
Your universe is boundless.
There is more than enough
of everything for everyone.

How does one take in the bounty that is there?
What does one do to deserve opulence?
You think this is not a difficulty?
Wait and see.

Until such a time when you have mastered
the art of receiving,
you must supply yourself
with the material necessities.

If you can release your guilt about money
and accept it as part of the Divine universe
and the physical reality of your earth,
you will see that it has no more or less power
than you give it.
It is a necessity.
You all hold the sense of money too tightly.

Sometimes I don't ask for "success"
on this physical plane
because it feels like I should find joy
in what is here and now
and I get confused
about wanting for myself.
Do you have any feelings on this?

I have very strong feelings on that.
There is a misconception
permeating spiritual practice
that says,
"You must want nothing in order to have everything."
If that is taken in the context
in which it was given,
the "want" that is referred to there is greed.

However, when there is desire
to taste the abundance of your world
and to receive it with love,
I see no reason at all
why you should not have it.

There is only conflict where you believe
there is a separation
between the bounty in your world
and the bounty of God's Love.

When you had a body
what did you do for a living, Emmanuel?

In my last incarnation, I was someone very like you
with one exception, in that I followed my heart
without one shred of guilt, regret or fear.
I became a teacher
and I walked around your world
and allowed myself to be touched with love
and I gave it back wherever I could.

I'll tell you something else:
I was rich, not perhaps in the coinage
that is so rigidly associated with wealth,
but I was rich
and I never went a day
without enough to eat.
I never went a night
without a wonderful place to sleep.
I had my home. I had my work.
And I had my integrity.

You dear souls walk so cautiously
as you enter the Garden of Eden.
Don't you know
that it's your rightful home?

There is such fear
when the thought of complete fulfillment
comes into your consciousness.
You are so identified with the seeking
that the finding becomes a threat.

Indeed, it is the most difficult thing
in the entire human experience—
to claim your Self, your Life, your Light,
your Truth and your God.

Every chance that you get along your way
sit in as much Light as you can.

Find as much joy and pleasure as you are able.
At no one's expense of course,
for that is not pleasure.
Push no one else out of the way, for that is pain.
But go where there is real pleasure:
the pleasure of self-recognition and love,
the pleasure of seeing another
with gentleness and compassion.
These are the real and abiding pleasures.
Physicality can be pleasurable.
Sexuality can be pleasurable—
when there is love.

The ultimate challenge to the illusion is love.
So love yourself.
Love others as you love yourself
(you certainly can't love any more than that)
because love is love.
And once it's there
it spreads out evenly in all directions.

Celebrate your life.
Bring pleasure into it wherever you can.
And see that pleasure as truth
not as some secret sin.
For if you judge pleasure
in the context of the illusion
then you lose the pleasure.
And it keeps you in the schoolroom longer.
It truly does. For you see,
suffering is not the way to Light and to Heaven.
Pleasure is.
Real pleasure. Not false pleasure.
And you all know the difference.
You all know when you fail yourselves.
You make yourselves sick.
You do foolish things. You become destructive.
Then you know you have betrayed yourselves.

When you begin to blossom and glow
and dance down the street
just because you are happy
and you know the illusion
is your creation,
here for your own education
and you can alter it anytime you want
simply by the act of self-love,
then you are free.
You are preparing your pathway Home
whenever you are ready to come.

In the meantime, you are teaching many others
the absolute truth of God's existence.
And you and I—all of us—
have a great deal of work to do.
But it is not to be arduous.
It is to be pleasure.
And when it is not, please don't feel noble.
Don't feel that somehow you are doing it right
because it is difficult.

*Stop at the very moment the pleasure leaves you
and say, "What have I forgotten?"
And if you are centered and in truth
the answer will be,
"Oh. I have forgotten that I am God."
Then you will take that remembering
back into your human experience
and you will dance again.
And we in spirit will dance with you.*

Then the task of fulfilling God's Plan of salvation
will go very quickly, for God is Love,
and pleasure is Love, and joy is Love,
and truth is Love. And all things are Light.
You will find that out
whether you believe me now or not.
Soon enough.
For you will grow through this lifetime
and you will age and you will die.
And I cannot imagine saying a more pleasant
and encouraging thing to you.
For if you were to remain in this illusion,
I cannot tell you how unhappy you would be
even though at the moment
you believe you really want to.

You will stay until your task is done,
until your lessons are learned.
And then we will all begin again
in some other dimension
to create in the name of God.

God bless you.

9
The Journey: Evolution, Reincarnation, Karma, Eternity

At any moment the heart can open.
At any moment the karmic structure
can be completely overcome
by the willingness of the soul.

The entire world is an illusion
spinning nicely through space
even though it does wobble a bit.
You accept the illusion
because you're good students
and you promised to come and to learn.
You promised to remain here in the illusion,
believing the illusion,
until what you have come to accomplish
has been done.
Then you can release it.

Now, what do I mean by that?
I mean that you have all signed a contract
before you agreed to be born again
that said, "Yes. I will enter this game
and I will agree to abide by all the rules."

That is necessary.
You know how difficult it is to learn
in even a human physical classroom
when you have refused to believe
that the teacher is the teacher
and that the blackboard is there to be written upon
and that what you are being taught has value.

So I am here not to promote rebellion
but to assure you
that what you are doing is valuable
and that what you are studying is necessary.
And yet, that the whole thing
is only a temporal illusion,
that your greater portion exists here
in the world of Light and Truth.
And that you *will* come Home.
You will come Home. I promise you.

**Why do we come into human form
and do so many, many times?**

Your existence in the limited human form
suggests the need for your consciousness
to have things in limited form.
As your development progresses
so does your vision expand
to encompass more and more of the universal truths
that exist within you now
as yet undiscovered.

The reincarnational wheel takes you round and round
until finally your resistance becomes so transparent,
so worn away through effort and experience,
that you can see the holes in it.
You no longer believe in its fabric.
You then put the limited, doubting mind
to the service of the heart.

All souls seeking their own identity
follow various forms of confusion
but it is a lighted path,
though it may seem to go through
terrible areas of darkness.

The purpose of the entire journey
is to find Truth
and then to return to Truth wiser
and better equipped to serve it
and ultimately to be it.

The very act of incarnation
is the statement of a soul's yearning
to become one again
with the Light.

As your awareness deepens,
the faster cause and effect come about
until the process of balancing is instantaneous.
Then there is no longer cause and effect.
There is only Truth.

How are our incarnations determined?

When a soul has achieved enough awareness to again
consider becoming human, then many wheels are set
in motion.

Before an incarnation all of the aspects of the soul's
needs and desires are profoundly studied. By whom?
By the soul itself and by the teachers and companions,
the loved ones that are not at that time encased in a
human form.

Since the purpose of human life is to learn and grow,
all manner of soul-design is incorporated, with great
creativity, into the projected human birth. The time
element, the cultural area, the sex, the race, the
family, the capacities—physical, mental and
emotional—are ordered. Not, perhaps, as one
might order a pizza, but utilized in the blueprint
of the soul.

Is reincarnation in linear time?

Where you are, yes.
Where I am, no.

Consciousness cannot help but create itself.
You must, by the very nature of your being,
expand and create.
Who you are at any given moment,
whether it be pre-birth, physical,
or after physical life,
is your creation.

The workshop of each lifetime
must be designed
to create the optimum environment
for learning.
All circumstances of infancy,
indeed the physical body itself,
are educational tools.

There are no mistakes in the reincarnational pattern,
though one may look with horror, and quite rightly so
(in your human stage of development), at misfortunes
that seem to befall those who were born in innocence.
There is no such thing as error here.

The Plan is perfect.
The design is exquisite.
And the nature of all reality
is love.

**Why do we have no memory
of past lives?**

You do.
You simply do not conceive of it as past life.
There is not one of you who, deep inside you,
is not aware of having been here before.

*You have already experienced all things.
You are only here now to remember that.*

**Does a soul
have choices for incarnation
other than the human earthly plane?**

As long as there is a need
for the physical earthly plane
this is where the soul will be.
Mind you, this is not the primary schoolroom.
There are others before you reach the earth.

When a soul has come to the realization
that reincarnation is to its best interest,
then the earth becomes a place of choice.
You will notice in the duality of your human world
that it is peculiarly designed for making choices.
A soul must be able to choose
in order to come into the world
and the soul that has completed
its reincarnational cycles
must have gotten to the point
where the ultimate choice has been made.

There is no hurry.
You are eternal.
If you forget something in this life,
there will be plenty of time again.

If you feel that you no longer wish
to be in your physical body,
question that
for you must come Home with love
not aversion or anxiety.
If there is a crumb of dissatisfaction
it will have to be swept up again in the future.

Your final incarnation is neat and tidy.
All the strings are tied.
All the corners dusted.
All the things are folded and put away.

**How difficult is it
for consciousness to obtain
a human body?**

In the beginning, it can be quite haphazard
as a soul crashes into this new dimension.
As one moves through the gamut of human experience
from one life to the next,
the choosing becomes more exacting.
In the ultimate incarnations
one must become more careful
and it may require a bit of waiting
but nothing as lengthy as centuries.

**Do we return
to lower forms of consciousness
if we stray from the path?**

That would not in any way serve the purpose
of the soul.

**Why did those six million souls
decide to come forth
to experience the Holocaust?**

The door that unlocks the soul
into incarnation
can fulfill many purposes;
teaching others
as well as self.
When a life is designed
to serve both ends
then the cause and the call
are magnificent.
At those times, the higher wisdom can say
"And this is necessary now."

One can sacrifice for others
and still have an excellent opportunity
to grow individually.
Of course, the path was chosen.
No one stumbles into such a thing.
Each soul is aware before birth of its needs
and of its ability to enhance its own growth
by contributing to the growth of others
in certain circumstances.

**Can a soul learn
from the type of fear
that is so pervasive
that there is no space
for understanding?**

The soul can learn.
Perhaps the human being can not.

**Did the whole process
of souls incarnating
begin at one time
or at different times
for each one of us?**

At different beginnings
for each one of us.
In the total Oneness of God,
eternal and ever-expanding,
all could not explode
into incarnation at once.
Each soul, in its own seeking,
carries with it its own time schedule.
As each consciousness expands and explores
and divides and becomes,
it carries within the moment
when it will desire to return.

It sounds a little chaotic.

You think it chaotic
because you think in terms of space
and in eternity
there is a lot of room.

**Is there a finite
number of souls?**

No, there is not.

**Where do new souls
come from?**

As consciousness expresses itself,
it divides and subdivides.
When it has divided to a point
where it no longer finds growth
or expanded awareness in division
then it begins to unify.
Ultimately, there will be one soul.

**At what point in human progress
does a soul no longer have to return
to the planet?**

When you have finally,
fully and completely,
recognized and experienced
your own Divinity.

**Are we living another life
simultaneously in another reality
parallel to the human?**

Yes, of course, many.

**Are these 'many' across time,
across space, across vibration?**

Across the board.

**Are all the incarnations
that we have ever had
all present at the same moment?**

To the center of consciousness
of the soul, yes.
You are a being of Light
and, from the Center of Light,
all things are now.
Yet, when that Light
enters into physical reality,
to that reality
there is chronology.

What does karma mean?

When I speak of karma
I am merely speaking of material to be transformed.
Karma is not a balancing of books.
There is a small part of every human being
that is resisting the will of God
or there would be no need
for the human experience at all.
Karma is a mode of learning.

Karma is the set of circumstances
that you have chosen to inhabit in this lifetime
in order to find the areas not yet in truth.
You are the creator of everything in your life.
Nothing happens that you have not called to you.
The inner desire of the wise and conscious soul
is to externalize,
to create a tangible manifestation
of what it internally holds to be true
and thereby experience that belief.
It is through that experience
that the transformation occurs.

**What if we make mistakes
or do unkind things?
Don't we have to pay
for them?**

You are not here to pay back or to be paid back.
You are here to grow.
In your willingness to grow
the karmic ties are released.
In the economy of God's Consciousness
what is no longer needed ceases to exist.

You have planted a garden
long before it has bloomed.
There are times when seeds that have been sown
need to come to flower
so that they can be recognized.
Then, consciously and with deep awareness,
they can be transplanted, nurtured or removed.
As you see in the present reality
crops that are not to your liking,
you must welcome them
as signs of past errors in judgement
coming into the light now
so that wiser choices can be made.

You are bound
by a structure of karmic significance
yet, as you go deeper and deeper
into your own inner wisdom,
that karmic structure is less and less confining.
It can be quickly transformed.

Although the karmic workshop
may seem to be a vast one,
no soul gives itself more work to do
than it is fully equipped to accomplish.

Karmic missions
are for self-forgiveness
and self-realization.

You do not stray and err because of deliberate denial
but only from fear, from ignorance,
and only to seek safety where safety is not.
You have become confused and separated
from your conscious connection with God.

Find your way back
through the labyrinth of your own human experience
and you will find the door is open
and the Light is there.

In those situations when one wilfully allows oneself
the God-denying act of harming another,
the soul is aware.
In one way or another it must
come to an understanding of that act.
It may take several lifetimes.
It may take a moment.

It might disappoint you to know
that you do not change drastically
once you have experienced
enough of the karmic realities
to move beyond your world.
You are still your own dear self.
Personally, I find that pleasant and remarkable.

This self that you defile and despise
and question and doubt and judge
and feel guilty about
is the very self
that will come Home with you. ⚘

**What happens to a soul
like Hitler or Stalin?**

When you say "a soul like Hitler or Stalin,"
I say to you
that you do not know their soul.
You may speak of a man like Hitler or Stalin
but you cannot speak of their total Divine Being.
There is a need in human consciousness
for retribution, for justice.
There are many things
that the human mind cannot understand.
You cannot will yourself
to forgive and love someone
who has seemingly caused such suffering.
From your viewpoint it is unforgivable.

There is a great deal of growth, certainly,
that needs to take place in souls,
not only those two, but anyone who is cruel,
who abuses, who kills, who is selfish,
who is ambitious, who is unfeeling.
It is a matter of degree.
Within each one of you there is a small portion,
some smaller than others,
where there is hate, where there is racism,
where there is a voice that says,
"I am different than you and I am better."
Wherever you can hear that voice,
you are speaking to what you have perceived
in the outer world as Hitler.

Remember, this is a schoolroom
and remember some of the lessons
need to be written across the heavens
in order for them to be heard
and understood.

**Did all consciousness evolve
through the more static,
simple forms of matter
into the more fluid
and complex?**

Those who have chosen the path away
have also chosen the path to return.
This involves the experience
of many different levels of consciousness.
As consciousness expresses itself,
it forms materially what you would term
many different levels of awareness
in your earth.
Yet it is always journeying back
to the Oneness.

If a portion of consciousness feels most comfortable
in creating itself as a rock, or a blade of grass,
this does not mean
that it is limited to that form.
It simply means
that a particular portion of the consciousness
can best serve its own needs
by experiencing that brief connection
to materialized reality
as a seemingly inanimate object. Simultaneously,
the consciousness may be creating itself
on other levels
including that of human existence.

As you begin to cherish the earth,
the song of a bird, the beauty of a flower,
and feel a oneness with it all,
what you are doing is releasing parts
of your frozen consciousness
to join again with that love light
that is your essential being.

A sense of oneness with all things of the earth
is a good indication
that you have claimed back into yourself
those portions that have evolved
through various experiences.
This leads to the total knowing of the earth
as one with your own being.
Literally, it is.

Do animals evolve?
Do they become people?

Of course.
Consciousness must create what it is
from the posture of its own existence.
When a consciousness expands,
it will grow to where it can reach
beyond its present understanding
into greater wisdom.

There is no end to evolution.
You, yourselves, will evolve
into beings far more brilliant,
far more beautiful
and far wiser.

**Can one graduate
ahead of schedule
from the curriculum
of life?**

There are no steps to be skipped.
The organic process cannot allow for that.
There would be holes where fear and doubt
and lack of faith would lurk
and it would all come tumbling down again
and you certainly do not want that.

You will find your path
and you will follow it to the end.
After all, this is not such a terrible place to be.
Have you not come to see the beauty and the ugliness,
the love and the hate, the light and the darkness?
Do not run from it.
Your task is to transform it
not to avoid it.

**Hey, Emmanuel,
what time is it?**

Now!

**If we are eternal,
what is the meaning of time?**

You speak of time. I speak of eternity.
Yet we both speak of the same thing
from different perspectives
of consciousness.

Time is an educational device.
Time is a necessary ingredient
for physical reality
for it provides a sense of structure,
a positive force
that helps you to stay focused
and related to the events of the schoolroom.
Anything that is designed
to keep the attention on the needed area
can be called a learning device.
When you have graduated
you will no longer need time
but until then you do.

Release yourself
from the confines of your physical body
and you are out of time
yet you are aware of being.

Where you are now
linear time is part of your environment.
When you go beyond the sense of time
as it is measured in your world,
time then ceases to be linear
and simply *is*.
It joins with the *is*-ness of all things.
You would not say that there is no time
but you would release it
from the conceptual bondage
of moving forward or backward
or of any reality
other than eternal beingness.

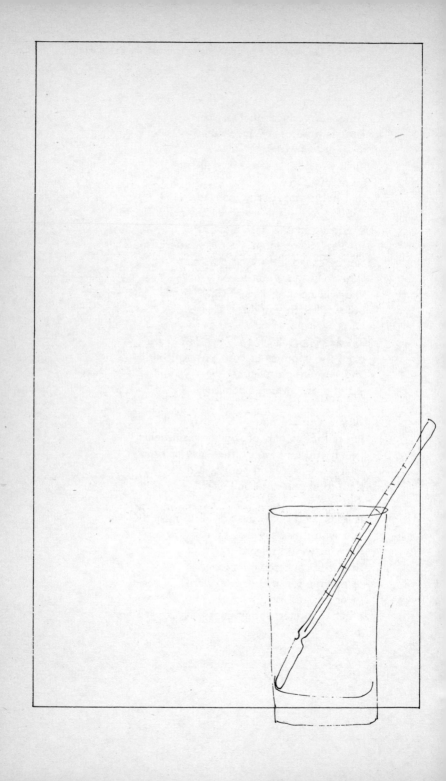

10
Illness and Healing

So much can be gathered
in that time of quietness, of introspection,
that illness forces upon you dear souls
who are always outer motivated.
Such times can be used
for the alchemy of taking the clay of physicality
and breathing the spirit into it
that will change that clay into gold. ❋

158

Illness is a teaching,
a message from the soul.
When the lessons are learned
the illness becomes
a thing of no moment.

Illness is the confusion of that particular soul
manifesting physically
so that the consciousness will see it.

Every part of an illness is you.
Listen to your body.
What is it saying?
Be that part of your body.
Once you have heard the voice
of those areas that are recalcitrant,
the mature mind can say,
"Let's find another way."
At that point, you quite literally
embrace that aberrated energy within you,
whether it is mental, physical or emotional,
and start to de-energize it
by simple acceptance of it.
The transformation begins.

Pain speaks to you
when you are ready to learn from it.
Emotional pain says one thing,
physical pain another.
Even its location in the body is eloquent.
Nothing in life happens haphazardly.
I realize that is a hard thing to hear
when someone is in pain
but the truth is the truth.
You live in a sane and ordered universe.
Make that your tenet.

Illness exists first
in the non-physical realm
of spiritual need,
emotional confusion,
or mental aberration.
It is never primarily physical.
The body is the reactor.
It vibrates to stress
and is an outward manifestation
of inner turmoil.

As the body constricts
under the onslaught of trauma,
there is a denial of energy
to a particular part of the body.
Thus the stage is set
for a physical manifestation
which is, in your reality,
a malfunction of the body.

Illnesses are classified
by their symptomatic manifestation
but their causes can be totally different.
The same illness
may exist in two different entities
for two different reasons.
It is the way that each body expresses
its outpicturing of disunity.

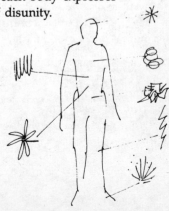

Are some illnesses karmic?

Karmic and stress are the same thing.
It is how you
have designed yourself in this life
to follow your soul's blueprint
into areas of conflict.
These can be termed karmic, and yet
that is a word that fosters more illusion
than clarity.

Healing can take place instantaneously
if there is recognition of the truth
of what has caused the illness.
So illness is, without exception,
a somatizing of that which the consciousness
has been unwilling to receive.

As the life force, the soul consciousness,
flows through the physical body,
those areas of the body that resist that life force
can develop a dysfunction at some point in life
depending on the needs of the soul.

Any denial is ultimately expressed in the physical
which is one of the reasons
people don physical bodies.
This way they must confront
what they are reluctant to confront
in the mental and emotional levels.

Your body in illness is not your enemy
but your faithful friend.
It has been programmed by your soul
to react in that exact way
at that exact time.
Do heed its guidance.

**Could the illness AIDS
be a plague from God?**

Oh, my dears, what a terrible thought
that God would ever send a plague.
How can we hope to heal this affliction
if we step aside and blame it on a deity?
No. No. You who recognize your autonomy
in your own lives
know full well that this is not the cause.

No God of loving compassion
would ever inflict upon anyone,
be it individual, group or community,
any illness at all,
not even the common cold.

If you believe
that you are deserving of punishment
you need to question
what you feel is amiss in your life.
Is there a sense of guilt?
Where you align yourself with any posture
that hints you are deserving of God's punishment
then that is the issue at hand.
Not the illness itself.

**Why are some of our bodies healthy
and others are crippled or diseased?**

You need to assume no guilt for a healthy body.
There is a reason for everything.
Know that you have learned in the past
the fortunes that are inherent
in a twisted and denied physical body.
Are you afraid that all things
are not distributed evenly
in God's universe?

Some people choose genetic factors
as they would buy a house with southern exposure
or a lake in the back.

They choose to inhabit a physical form
that has a potential for a specific disease
as a release valve.
It is designed to react in that way
when certain elements in their life
come to a point
where they do not care to go any further.

**Are insane people
consciously in control
of their insanity?**

No.
They are spiritually in control of their insanity.
But to say that one controls one's insanity
is to make a cruel statement.

There is also the school of belief,
quite true,
that insanity is a wise decision
where there have been circumstances or trauma
with which the human being
is simply ill-equipped to cope.
Indeed, insanity is a healing.

The soul, which is the crux of the question,
is aware
but the soul has committed itself to growth
in that human life
and often not only for its own sake
but for the contribution to the learning experience
of others. ❀

If we could launder the word "cancer,"
hang it out in the sun to dry
and bring it in bleached white and beautiful,
I promise you that there would be less cancer
and less death from it.
Souls would choose other ways.

The issue of cancer is the issue of fear—
cancer brings a message of fear—
that is so prevalent in all your world.
And so the illness must be dealt with squarely
as fear.

Once cancer is cured
there will be something else.
People have to deal with fear
because it is one of the greatest denials
of the reality of God.

I have been told
that there is no illness
that cannot be cured.
Trusting this,
what can I do
to regain my health?

There is an issue of will here.
When one says
"There is nothing that cannot be cured,"
there is an insistence that says,
"on my terms."

Is there truly a cure for all illness?
I would say yes, if you would be wise enough
to consider death a cure.

The body knows, in its infinite wisdom,
what is needed for equilibrium.
You are your own diagnostician
and your own doctor, if you will but listen.

Let me tell you
that when the soul is ready to leave the body
you could be walking around
as a strong and healthy athlete
and the heart would stop.
If the soul is not ready to leave
the body will heal itself.

You need to recognize the power
of the liberated consciousness of the human being—
not the will, but the liberated consciousness—
that has the ability to reconstruct and heal
its own body.

As some of you
will evolve in your lives to be healers,
let me remind you that there are some souls
that do not wish to be healed.

"You must be healed,"
is so often the message that is given
with the healing.
No, they must not be healed.
Only if they want to.
And you are not the authority on that.
Do not inflict your will.

Just give love.
The soul will take that love
and put it where it can best be used.

**Can people heal others
by the laying on of hands?**

Through the connection of two or more
who are gathered in the name of Truth and Light,
the love force enters
and alters the body chemistry and energy systems
of the one who is ill.

It only takes two,
with love and openness and trust,
to create remarkable circumstances—
two and the Divine Spirit.

By absent healing?

If you send someone healing
let it be a prayer
that they accept their illness
and allow it to bring
whatever wisdom is intended.

An ultimate form of healing
which is an evolved state
that may not come into your human world
for another two thousand years
involves the treatment of ailing bodies
with pure water.
The effectiveness of this treatment
will rest on faith.

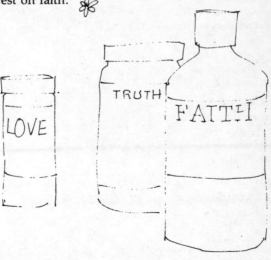

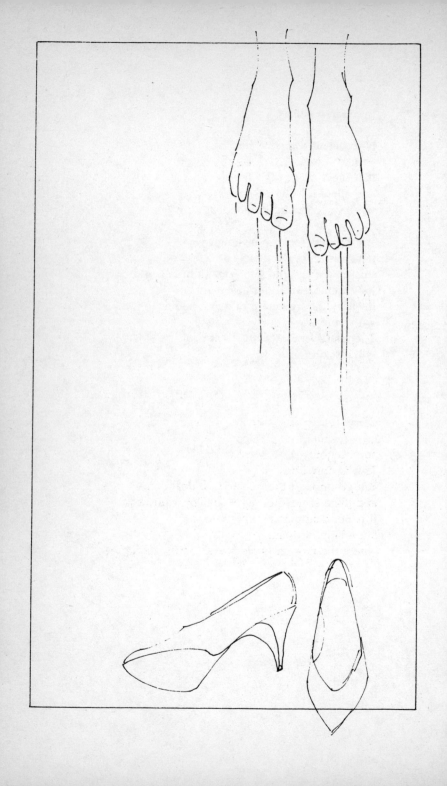

11
Death

Death is like taking off a tight shoe.

Even when you are dead,
you are still alive.
You do not cease to exist at death.
That is only illusion.
You go through the doorway of death alive
and there is no altering of the consciousness.
It is not a strange land you go to
but a land of living reality
where the growth process is a continuation.

Life and death
should not be considered as opposites.
It is closer to the truth
to speak of dying as an entrance
rather than an exit.

What the doorway of death offers
is a resurgence of tremendous vitality,
for you are entering from what could be described
as a watered down version of life
into the thing itself,
the vitality of the primary reality.

If death could be seen
as a beautiful clear lake,
refreshing and bouyant,
then when a consciousness
moves towards its exit from a body,
there would be that delightful plunge
and it would simply swim away. ✳

Dying is self-regulating.
It is of Divine origin.
It is absolutely safe.
The fear of death
is the fear of letting go.
As it is in life,
so it is in death.
The process of dying
is always a joyous one
once the human fear has been overcome.
When fear is laid aside,
death becomes a most exciting adventure.
There is nothing to fear in the universe.
Nothing.

When souls leave physical bodies,
as in a profound meditation,
there is a light,
a sense of well-being,
of peace, and of knowing
that you are there in your entirety,
in your individuality.
You have not ceased to exist
but have gone into another level
of more intense existence.

It is important to remain vitally alive
in the decision-making process
during the final act of completion
in physical life.
It is an excitement
like packing the bags
to go on a long-awaited trip.

Death is only a passage through,
a time of release.
Dying is no different than living.
Once you are filled with a sense of Self
you know that you exist beyond death.
One of the first joys of release
is the reconstruction of the image of Self
into the Oneness of all things,
without for one moment losing the Self.
I, myself, am a product
of the after-death experience.

Why would anyone desire to remain
in physical reality
when their task is finished
and they are approaching Light?
Think about it.
It is often a mystery to us,
even when we have been human
and remember the fear.
It is difficult to really comprehend
the tenacity with which someone will cling
to a decaying and useless form
when such joy and Light await
at the exit door.

We are always there to welcome
those who exit
so leave your bodies
with arms spread
to receive the embrace.

No soul passing into primary reality
goes unattended.
If you leave so suddenly
that you may not realize your actual condition,
you would need to see some being who looks
human.
If you just saw spirit at that moment,
you would not be as comfortable.

There are those of us who have volunteered,
enlisted as it were,
to provide the soul when it is released from the body
with a focal point
to assist in orientation
to the new state of being.

Once the soul is oriented, the Guides will appear.
What is seen depends on the belief system.
It may be a lighted Buddha,
a lighted Christ,
or another holy figure,
but it will be Light.
The soul will then be led to where it needs to go
and where, at the deepest level of being,
it wants to go.

I had thought I was a conscious being.
How come, then, I was so terrified
when I thought I might die?

Because, my dear friend,
you are also human
and because the portion of you
that must die when you do
does not want to.
It is the portion that says,
"I am a personality. I am a human being
in this physical world.
The self that I have struggled so hard to defend
deserves eternity. I do not wish
to take that step into the unknown
because unknown things frighten me."

That's all right. That does not mean
that the greater portion of you is not enlightened.
It is. But do not force enlightenment
on the part of you that cannot contain it.
Allow that part to remain human.
Comfort it.

Your higher wisdom is ready
at any time
to take that terror into its arms
and to lull it, to cradle it,
to caress it into the blissful state of death.

What a cruel statement,
"I thought I was enlightened
and here I am afraid!"
Can you not see
that in your world of duality
this is quite appropriate?

**Will we ever be able
to increase the life span of the body,
perhaps to where death could be overcome?**

What in the world would you want to do that for?
I honestly cannot think of anything more unpleasant
than to remain forever locked in your schoolroom.
The only purpose for that might be to allay fear.
The purpose of life is to grow through fear
and show its flimsy nature.

Life will extend by its own volition
if your soul has not finished what it has come to do.
*You are here to visit
not to remain.
This is not a curse.
It is a gift from God.*

**What does it actually feel like
while we're dying?**

Dying is akin to having been in a rather stuffy room
where too many people are talking and smoking
and suddenly you see a door that allows you to exit
into fresh air and sunlight.
Truly it is much like that.

Matter becomes less dense.
Consciousness becomes less restricted.
Colors become more vibrant.
Sounds become more pleasant.
All the senses, finally released
from the heavy cloak of the physical body
take flight with song.

When one claims back to oneself the energies,
those consciousnesses
that have inhabited the physical body,
one does very much what God does.
One says to the cells,
"You no longer need to exist
in the molecular structure of my spleen,
so come and dwell with me
in my larger Self
until such a time as, for the good of all,
we must again inhabit a human form."

**What do we experience
immediately after death?**

*There are as many individual ways
to leave a body
as there are to live in one.*
Why would it be supposed
that one's creative ability ceases
at the moment consciousness leaves the physical?

When there is a reaching and yearning for Light,
for love, and for the touch of a beloved hand,
then this is what is experienced.
When there is a belief that all will be lost,
then unfortunately, this must be experienced too
for a brief period of time.
One is not allowed to remain overlong
in one's own creation.
Having left the body is quite enough.

The instant that the Self
releases from the human body,
there is Light, there is peace,
there is freedom, there is Home.

If I could show you in tangible form
the circle that is your world's consciousness
and let you see the Light
that surrounds that world,
you would never again question
the comfort and caring that is experienced
the moment you leave the circle
of human limitation.

You are allowed to rest, to sit quietly
and bask in the awareness
of the continuing and eternal Self.
Those who are ready will instantaneously meet
with their teachers and old friends whom they love
to celebrate a most joyous reunion.
Yes, quite like human beings.
Do not forget that you have formed around you
something that is not alien to your consciousness,
for consciousness must create itself.
As you find yourself in your own Beingness,
you will also recognize yourself
without your physical body.

There may also be a time for healing
and many do, indeed, fall into a profound sleep.
They waken gently when they can sense
the safety and love that surrounds them.
Others rush joyously into the new existence.
Most beings, I am pleased to say,
find the transition instantaneously pleasurable.

After physical death, for most of you,
there follows a period
in which the fears and confusions
and resistances of human life
need to be understood
from the point of view of eternity.

Having successfully entered
into the fresh air again, if you will,
to the primary reality
where you belong through eternity,
you will eventually find yourselves
becoming curious, beginning to stretch,
as after a long vacation.
Suddenly you know full well it is time
to stand up and begin to move.
Often, indeed in most cases,
there is a renewal of interest in human life
for you have left behind unfinished business.
So it is back to the womb
but only after deep consideration.

**What would it be like
at the moment of death
if we are ready
to turn fully into the Light?**

The moment does not come as a surprise.
One is aware, while still human,
of that moment of turning.
It is the willingness to touch with love
all things of the human earth
and yet loving them enough to release them,
knowing that on the releasing
there is no loss.
There is only an altering of consciousness
into a deeper Oneness.

The Light is sensed and known
before it is perceived.
At that point of turning,
of surrender with deepest trust
and with the sharpest pinpoint awareness,
one leaves the physical
and turns directly into the Light.
One has already turned halfway around
before the body is left.

**And at that moment
are the One and the total uniqueness
simultaneously present?**

Yes, and forever after that.

If, in a lifetime, you find within your heart
the wisdom to forgive yourself
for your human imperfections,
there is a great possibility
that your death will be instantaneous
and extremely comfortable.

One can leave peacefully in sleep
if all things are balanced
and in accordance with the soul's desires.
Mind you, I did not say "if one is totally evolved,"
for each life has a capacity
and when that capacity is reached
then one can leave in peace.
Though others say, "They died most beautifully
and peacefully in their sleep
but they were not evolved,
they didn't do this and they didn't do that,"
you have no way of knowing
what the soul's task was in this life.
If the task has been completed
the life will end thusly.

Now, many die through long and extreme illnesses.
And this does not mean
that they have not accomplished
their soul's determination.
It only means
that they are doing so as they leave.

*To be vibrantly alive to your moment of
death is to grow to the fullest possible
extent in a lifetime.*

The soul chooses
whatever is most worthy of its process at that time.
It may be to help others grow
or to linger in the body
so that its own consciousness can continue to evolve.
Perhaps the soul will decide to leave most hastily
so as to grow from the other side of physical life
by reevaluating the needless fears
that had haunted it up to the time
of the sudden death.

Death is nothing to be apprehensive about.
It is just part of a process
that you have been involved in for centuries.
You are not at the edge of an abyss.
You are merely taking another step
in your eternal existence.
Souls need ways to get out of bodies when ready.
My dears, why do you tremble so?
Death is a swinging door.

My brother committed suicide.
What do I need to know about this?

Your brother took his life and brought it Home.
Although the inadvisability of suicide is spoken of,
it is all right.
It is clear that when one chooses to quit school
it is necessary to come back again
and learn what could not be learned at that time.
I speak to you from eternity
and there is no limit
to the number of lives one can have.

Your brother is learning many valuable things.
He is Home. He is well.
He is working, and will design a curriculum
next time that will be more compatible
with his willingness and his needs.

It is to yourself
that you must direct your attention.
What does it mean to you
to have a brother who killed himself?
You need to hear the voice of God within you
which knows it's all right,
that he is eternal.
Hear the message he gave you.
No one acts alone.
No one acts in a vacuum.
No one kills himself
without leaving a legacy of growth behind.

There is no punishment in God.
There is only eternal love and understanding.
Suicide is merely a foolish act
and as such it reaps its own reward—
and there you are.

Your prayers and blessings
will be much appreciated,
but more than that,
your gentle, sweet and smiling understanding
of the futility of the act
will be most welcome.

Why does someone die
when they're very young?

Because they have completed their task.
There is no other reason.
Young?
You are all eternal.
Once you escape
from the time-space continuum,
that 'young'
becomes a very old soul.

On accidental death:

There is no such thing as an accident.
When your soul chooses to leave your physical body
it will leave.
Life is not an amateur circus tent
where those who enter
are individual, lonely performers
with no script and no director—
only a tumbling about,
a fling through the air,
and then a crash.
No. That is false.

As souls, you are self-determining.
You decide when to be born.
You create your life
every minute of every day
by what you choose to believe.
You decide when to die.
All things evolve
around the total truth of love,
balance, order, cause and effect.
These are Divine laws.

**After death
are there different levels
for souls?**

Are there not within your own human realm
levels of awareness?
Would it not then follow
that in the realm of spirit
there are also varying levels?
We are not speaking of the value of a consciousness
but as you climb the ladder of your awareness
you follow your own blueprint
of the nature of reality
both in your realm and mine.
It is one reality.
The only difference
that separates you from me at this moment
is that you believe
in what your five senses are now registering.
You accept their power to limit you.
The moment that you stretch beyond that belief
you are home free.

**How do we prepare
for the loss of loved ones,
or can we?**

There are two answers.
Loved ones are never lost, and you can't.
You must experience it in your own way.
Of course, you will miss the physical being
but when you learn to go beyond that,
there will be no missing at all.
Even as you sit in your human form,
once you allow yourselves—
notice the word 'allow'—
to believe that you exist beyond the physical,
you will touch hands with those who have left.
And it will be real.
It will be more real
than the physicality that you had touched before.

Are you aware that the physical body
is a shield or a shell?
It does not reveal
but rather hinders revelation.
If you did not have need of illusion
you would not need a physical body at all.

**Do you have suggestions or instructions
for those left behind
as to what they should do
immediately following
the death of a loved one?**

That is an excellent question.
First, the willingness to let that person
go into the next step of their evolution
is extremely helpful, not only to you but to them.
A "farewell," a "bon voyage," a "Godspeed."
Then the rest of you look at each other
and give comfort and assurance, and the hugs
and the kleenex that is necessary.
Next, take yourselves to a place of great luxury
and enjoy an incredible feast.
Salute the soul that has completed its task,
touch glasses to the time when you will meet again
and go about the business of your own lives.

*Death is not only a time of mourning.
It is a time of truth.*

Karmic ties can be formed
by an unwillingness to express any negativity
thus holding resentments
that go into the soul consciousness
to return in another life.
By your dealing with the negative emotion,
by cleansing the relationship,
you are helping both of you.

"Don't speak ill of the dead."
That's nonsense.
There is no such thing as "the dead"
in the first place, and the belief
that the dead must be protected
goes against reality.
In their lifted state of consciousness
they are better able to hear the truth.

Communication does not stop
at the doorway of death.
The wall between physical reality
and spirit reality is very thin,
as you can see by the fact
that I am standing here talking with you.

You, in your element,
and the person who has died, in his or her element,
can work on the same issues
and come to a deeper understanding
even though the illusion
says you are totally separated.
Your truth can propel the lifted one into growth.
Quite the opposite from what most people believe.

**When we send messages of love
to one who has died,
how can we know
if the loved one
has received them?**

By knowing the nature of love
which is the eternal power of the universe.
When it is expressed and sent,
love is instantaneously received.

Whether the receiver is exactly the same person
that you remember is another matter.
Growth continues.
Even though it is most comforting to recall
someone as you last knew them, it is guaranteed
that there has been a change for the positive
even as you think of them.
*There is something remarkably refreshing
and educating about dying.*

Someone who found it difficult to say,
"I love you. Thank you
for sharing your life with me,"
would be willing to acknowledge those feelings
once he or she has removed themselves
from the physical body.
I do not mean that instantly everyone is wise,
merely more aware.

**You speak of expanded consciousness
that exists after death. Doesn't individuality
necessarily have some eventual end?**

Is there a time when all blends into one?
Yes.
But there is never a time
when one blends into nothingness.

12
Relationship:
Marriage and Divorce,
Family, Sexuality

The purpose of human love
is to awaken love for God.

The doorway of human love
is a perfectly acceptable channel
to experience the broader realities,
for love is love.

As you learn to love
you open to the very act of loving itself.
That love is given to the world in many ways.

The opening of your heart
whether to another human being,
an animal, community involvement,
or a relationship with your environment,
is still an opening to love.

191

Throughout human history,
and there have been many human histories,
the interpersonal relationship between
a man and a woman
has required many different things.

What is most essential today
is honesty, truth, and love.
Truth and love cannot be separated.
They walk hand in hand.

When one doubts one's lovableness
then truth seems to be anathema to safety.
But when one becomes assured
that one is, indeed,
the light of truth and beauty,
desirability and sweetness,
then self-exposure becomes
a thing of pleasure
rather than terror.
Then the interpersonal relationship
can deepen and ever deepen
to a wondrous oneness.

**On relationships
between men and women:**

In this human world
where duality is the language of the text,
see the male and female
not as eternally separate, but as parts of you
that you have chosen to manifest.
You are not strangers to each other.
You are only parts of each other.
The part that you choose to inhabit
will be one or the other
because that is the nature of your human world.
Thus relationship between a man and a woman
is just another way of seeking Self.

*Human love
is not a substitute for spiritual love.
It is an extension of it.*

*Each lifetime
and each relationship within each lifetime
is an opportunity to experience love.*
When you see each other
as the Divine and eternal beings that you are,
you will never cease to wonder and to glory
in the coming together. Do not be seduced
into seeing each other merely as the human shell.
Rather, see the soul, the consciousness within.

Soul mate.
Now there's a subject
that one could go on and on about.
When one is speaking to ultimate truth
there is no one in human existence
who is not your soul mate.

Strangers on the other side of the world,
at the roots of their being,
are one with you and you with them.
If only this realization
could be fostered throughout your planet,
there would never be another war,
there would never be another clash
of harmful, destructive nature
anywhere.

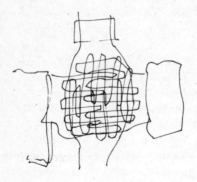

**If one longs for a mate,
is it best to seek this relationship,
to wait for it to happen
or to try to cultivate detachment
as one waits for it to happen?**

The last, not at all.
If you become detached from your desire,
your desire will never be fulfilled.
It will simply remain an appendage
that weighs you down and causes you pain.

Though you consciously long for a mate,
there are parts of you that do not,
that push the idea away,
that hasten to lock the door
when the other part of you
has so carefully opened it.
Look around. Do a little house cleaning
and you will see where it is you still fear,
reject, deny, criticize and judge
those parts of you
that long for physical and emotional intimacy.
Once the space is ready
the mate will be there.

Think about that.
Then buy yourself the most magnificent outfit
and begin to dance.

The more you align yourself
with your own integrity
the more you will seek Oneness with God
and will then be able to accept
that infinite, outrageous, and terrible love
that says you and I are One.

**Does the male-female polarity
we have on this physical plane
exist in the spirit realm?**

In the world of unity
there is no polarity.
The male-female aspects are self-united.
No one truly is more male than female
or more female than male.

**Then is there sexuality
in the spirit world?**

If by 'sexuality' you mean the feeling of oneness,
of light and love, of boundaryless blending,
oh yes. But it has been removed
from physical sexuality
and taken completely into the heart.
We have learned the lessons
that separation in physicality offer
and we no longer require that.

How do you use your heart
to choose a relationship
when your heart seems pulled
in two different directions?

At the risk of sounding hedonistic,
why don't you follow them both?
In truth, when one is so determined to find
the one eternal relationship,
there is a weightiness
that comes about the heart
that disavows its own wisdom.
Be careful of this.
Be joyous and celebrate love
wherever it beckons you.
How would you know truth from falsity
if you had never tasted falsity?

There are many incarnations
in which there is no place or reason
for the one ultimate relationship.
Remember, my dears, this is not heaven.
It is a way to heaven.
Be willing to accept limitation without mourning.
You are in a finite world.

**Why are so many marriages
ending in divorce?**

It is because people have accelerated
their growth processes.
Souls come together, not to remain together
in physical contact, but to grow.
When this has taken place
the gifts have been given
and the lessons have been learned.
So don't you agree that it's time to move on?

All things are in order.
Do not be alarmed by change.
Things are speeding up
not to leap into the pit of destruction
but to come to that plateau of understanding
that you are seeking.

**What can I do
concerning my deteriorating marriage?**

Let it deteriorate.
Marriage is another word for relationship
and when a relationship no longer serves,
if you have scraped the bottom of the barrel
to find the meaning, to find the lessons,
to find the essence of why you have come together,
and this has not brought forth
what you are seeking,
what more can you possibly do?

If there is no true wedding
it matters very little how you close it.

Can you not let this go
with your love and your blessings
so the next time you meet this soul again
there will be more compatibility,
more compassion, more understanding?
For you will meet again.
Since all will ultimately come to Oneness,
there is not one person you encounter in your life
you will not see again.
Think about that.

**How can I know
when it may be time
to leave a painful relationship?**

When you have had quite enough of pain.
If, because someone else finds another turn
in the path that they must take,
you feel somehow diminished,
you have not found your own dimension.
You have only found identification with another.

On open marriage:

Each one must choose how they will experience life.
I think to say 'open' and 'marriage'
is to contradict oneself.

*The meaning of marriage, as I have perceived it,,
is that it is the coming together
with integrity and commitment,
to honor the God within each other
and to foster the greatest possible growth.*
How an open marriage can contribute to this
I fail to see.
It scatters the focus that belongs to the one.

No, I am not puritanical.
Where there is a proclivity to intermingle
with others outside your marriage,
I say that is entirely up to you.
But be aware
that you are dissipating a great treasure.

When you dissipate it,
it is not only that you give less
but you also receive less.
One does not receive an ounce more
than one gives
so ultimately what you are doing
is denying yourself
the abundance you seek in many places
rather than building it in one.

Now, if a marriage itself is not compatible
then I don't know what you would be doing there
in the first place.
If you have joined in union and find
that you have grown in different directions,
well, hooray for both of you.
Be blessed and joyous
and move to more compatible surroundings.
But where there is a commitment
and the commitment wishes to remain so,
I cannot see why that is not enough.

**Our marriage seems boring and stuck
although we still love each other.
What can we do?**

The first step is to acknowledge that. You are aware
that not only have you slowed to a stop
in your relationship, but there is still love.
When that love is truly accepted
you will find a way to unstick yourselves.

Love is not something that can be talked about
and then not honored.
Love is the deepest reality
that exists in the universe.
One does not casually say, "Well the love is there,"
and then continue
the same old destructive patterns.

You must first
place on the altar of your relationship
the ember of your love.
You will find a means
to fan it into flame again
by therapeutic methods, by prayer,
by physical activities, by whatever is possible
in your human world.
But first the love.

Be very careful, my dears, when you say,
"Of course I love you."
Be sure you know what you mean
for one sometimes says 'love' as a defense
or to hide from one's own unlovingness.
Love can be spoken
in order not to experience it.

Because love
is the most powerful force in the universe
it is also the most frightening
until it has been entered into completely.
That generally happens
just about at the finishing point
of the final life.

Do not become enamored of the boredom.
It is not as safe as you think it is.

**How does sexuality
relate to spirituality?**

Love is often felt as sexuality.
Your body is an instrument of experience.
When you experience love,
you do so in your total physical being.
There is nothing within you dear souls
that is not designed to express love.

Sexuality is a wonderful door to oneness.
It is the willingness to see and to be seen,
to share as completely as you are able
through each and every part of your dear self
so that you can be known and cherished.

There is a necessity in the human committment
to honor the reality of the sexual union.
It is, perhaps, the most direct means of unification
when it is experienced on all levels,
not only at the physical, of course,
but not only at the spiritual either.
Be careful of that, for you are all things
and you exist on all levels.

Sexuality is a biological doorway into truth.

**What role
does homosexuality play
in human relationship?**

*A necessary one.
It is a means of loving.
It is a means of reaching for oneness.
It is a means to camouflage fear.
It is, in short, a path.*

It is difficult to accept unification
because you live in a world
that encourages the either-or illusion.
But things are becoming more closely aligned.
Many people are learning to accept
their androgynous natures.
Some express it in homosexuality,
which is an overstatement, however,
because of the need to accept
the sexual structure of the physical world.
Nevertheless, in the long run
it is a healthy statement in your civilization.

Ultimately we are all androgynous.

The family
is a hothouse for spiritual growth.

It is impossible to avoid realization
and growth in the family situation.
That is why the institution of family
was incorporated into the earthly design.

The entrance of children into a family
is catalytic
for they are imbued with many unknown attributes
that exist within the parents.
This is known to the soul
and is part of the gift it brings—
an opportunity for the parents to see
at a more visible level
what it is they carry within themselves.

See children as shining, lighted mirrors of God
and of you human beings who have spawned them.
They may also be the painful reflection
of the inner architecture of their parents.
How they reflect is their own souls' process.

They are there to be loved, cherished,
guided, protected, nurtured and released.

On parenting:

Love is the purpose of parenting.
There is the need to teach.
There is the need to comfort, to guide,
but never for one moment must there be
the sense of superiority or separateness.

Your children have chosen you
because they know you.
More often than not
you have been together before
in different family configurations.

Communicate clearly with love, honesty,
truth, a willingness to be seen
and with compassion and wisdom
to the best of your capacity.
That will best serve
the soul purpose of your children.

The only gift that anyone has to give
is the self.
I cannot imagine a more beautiful,
beautiful presentation.

My daughter is using drugs.
Can you offer a perspective
and an avenue for help?

That which seems to be so harmful
and, indeed, in the physical form is so,
is not the ultimate destruction.
There is no such thing in God's Consciousness.
There is learning, and that is all.

It would be well to address this issue
by asking yourself
what are you to learn from this.
Why is this offered to *you?*
Not from a sense of victimization
but from a sense of gratitude.
What is it that you are experiencing?
What is it that you fear?
Where is it that you find the hidden resources?
Where is it that you collude, and so forth?
Judgements at this time have no value at all.
They simply close the door more tightly
to the avenue of healing.

No one exists alone in the world.
Your child is not alone
and so you are part of her decision
to exit from reality
through the doorway of drugs.
I do not say this to burden you with guilt
but to urge you to take up your part
in this interaction.
Children offer fulfillment
of what parents have failed to give themselves.
See where this mirrors you and be willing
to accept that with love and with grace.

All mothers are loved ones
that you have known before.
There is no deeper relationship
on the physical planet
than mother and child.

This does not in any way intend to negate
the position of fathers.
I can only comfort fathers by saying
you were mothers, too, and you are children now
so there is still the closeness, the bonding.

Once there is the bonding
there is never separation.
Once there is love
there is always oneness
even though lifetimes may go by
where you do not find yourselves
in physical form together.
I might say that when such affection
has already been experienced, you may meet
in the world of spirit during dreams.

**What is my responsibility
to my mother
in her illness?**

Because someone is ill
does not mean that they must be the altar
upon which you sacrifice your life.
If your truth is to be with her
then it is not a duty.
It is a fulfillment and a joy.
If it is not your truth to be with her
then you must follow your heart.
Don't you see, my dears,
in your innermost truth you can do no wrong.

**Is it possible
to communicate with animals?**

When you feel, with opening hearts,
a brotherhood
of communication with different species
then you are touching the seeds
that have created your earth.

When you allow that
to become the truth of your very breath,
all life will speak to you.

As you surrender to the ultimate reality
that all life *is* love, manifesting *in* love
and therefore One,
you will find
that on that line of communication
all consciousness knows itself.

**Can dolphins
speak to us?**

In the animal world
a dolphin expresses its love and awareness
by simply being who it is.

A dolphin has seen great Light
and feels great love
and now wishes to reach out
to share such love.
The consciousness of love within this being
is seeking a place to express itself.
Love is a gift that must be given.

When a dolphin is asked to communicate
in thought patterns similar to human's
you are pressing it to emerge
from its place of beingness too quickly
for its best interests.
Oh, my friends, can you not let things
speak to you in their own language?

13
Issues of This Time and Place: Survival of the Planet, War, Government, Abortion, Child Abuse, The Holocaust

Do not believe for one moment
that your birth is an accident
or that your world is a fumbling hodgepodge
of chaos and confusion.
It may seem so from the limited viewpoint
of human perspective, but I promise you
that all things are in order
and that in good time God's work
will become clear to everyone.

As the curtain lifts and your awareness expands
you will see your entire planet
as a cathedral of Light dedicated to God.
Each one of you holds within
the sceptre of your own infinite power.

**What is the meaning
of these turbulent times?**

You tend to lose sight of the purpose of life.
What better background for introspection,
for exploring one's own true beliefs,
for following one's own light and sharing it,
than at times of seeming crises and peril.
*What a wondrous backdrop
for inner confrontation, for growth.*

There is much to enlighten, to give hope
and a sense of rightful pride
in the process and progress of humanity.
This focus on what seems to be eminent stupidity
finally conquering the world
does a disservice to the whole.
Most certainly, acts of cruelty, viciousness,
childishness will continue to exist
as long as your schoolroom exists
but there is little reason to believe
that this is all that humankind consists of.

Do not become lost in assuming
that your world is a reasonable place.
Of course it is not reasonable.
It is a reflection of struggle.
Of course it is not gentle and fair
until one rises to the consciousness
within your own being
that cherishes gentleness and fairness.

**Is our planet
on the edge of destruction?**

School cannot be dismissed so early.
The bell will not ring.
You will not go on the extended vacation
that many are seeking by saying
"Let's get it over with."

Man is still so immature
that in believing himself powerful enough
to obliterate the world
there is a sense of grandiosity
that borders on the infantile.
This immaturity gravitates to the false promise
of absolute power that negativity extends.
There is no such thing in your world
as absolute power, even in limited form.

*Look within yourselves
as to where the satisfaction of an Armageddon
might be lurking.*

The inappropriateness of such destruction
is self-evident to everyone on your planet.
Why, then, do you suppose
it would be less obviously inappropriate
to the All-Seeing Consciousness of Love?
You have been schooled too severely
in the thinking of your human earth
that says that if I am angry at you
and you are angry at me
then what must ensue
is a raging battle.

Although there are those who are raging willy-nilly
to bring the world
to the edge of destruction and beyond,
there is also, within those same beings,
the consciousness of Light seeking Light.
Though their path may seem to be abhorrent
it is, after all, a path.

Though I certainly would not say to you
"Isn't the endless stockpiling
of nuclear weapons marvelous?"
I would say to you, "My dears,
trust the wisdom of the universe
and trust each being
that exists in your human world with you."

If you who are seeking love and truth
cannot rise above the illusion of turmoil,
how can those who are locked in it be helped?
It is you who are empowered
through the strength of your love,
your commitment to truth,
who will bring about the elevation of consciousness
of those who are wracked in such fear
that they would destroy the world
rather than acknowledge their own terror.

The purpose of life
is not to be shielded from one another.
There is the most intense necessity
to learn to love.
Even the earth's pollution
is a means of learning to care
and that in itself
will alter what is happening.

Do not wash your hands of the earth.
It has many good years left.
The human race does not have to be dismissed
from its schoolroom through a holocaust.
There can be a gentler coming Home
than the ones that some of you have imagined.
But yes, there will come a time—
science is quite right—
when your planet will dissolve.
Not in your lifetimes.
But when you have all completed the schooling
the earth can go Home.
It will return to Light.

Don't you think it will have earned it by then,
having been stamped upon, drilled into, hammered at,
distrusted, toxified? Don't you think it deserves
a little rest, just as you do,
after a long and useful life?

Let your physicality go when your time comes.
It's earned it.
That part of the consciousness deserves
to be returned to Light.
And so do you.

I would like to share a few thoughts on the subject of ecological balance.

This may appeal to many who are touching the awareness of their own contribution to the entity earth and the creatures thereon. There are many others who will find little connection between some of the other points of discussion and the rather earthy subject of the substance upon which you stand, the food that you eat and the air that you breathe. You may ask, "Well, if I am a soul and I am here to learn, then why do I have to be at all concerned with those circumstances that have existed before I was born and will most certainly continue to exist after I have taken myself out of this rather soiled and seedy world and have moved to other areas of consciousness?"

The only answer that can be given to such a question is that the world is a mirror and the more one polishes and cleans the mirror, the better one can see one's reflection. Since the essence, the purpose of life, is self-discovery, then does it not stand to reason that the elements that are used in this magnificent venture need to be kept in tip-top condition? It might be viewed as a selfish thing, perhaps, but it most certainly lends itself to the good of all.

**Why didn't we create a world
that was a shiny mirror
in the first place?**

Because you have come to see
in this particular mirror,
your own cloudiness as well as your own Light.
When you can see
through the pollution and the carelessness,
the wonderful beauty of your home,
when you can touch with love
beyond the tarnished outer reality,
you will revitalize what exists within
and the earth will truly shine again.

*The nature of the physical material
in which you associate and work is reflective.
Everything you touch reflects.
As long as there is one soul adrift
in the sea of infinite consciousness,
the earth will not assume its rightful clarity
for that soul will see its own reflection
and thereby smudge the perfect mirror.
It must be so.*

**Is there cosmic significance
to the strange weather
we've been having?**

Do not read disaster into natural phenomena.
The earth is very wise.
She is simply balancing her ecology.

**How should we
view the threat
of nuclear power?**

Without fear.
Do not fear nuclear power per se.
It is part of God's universe.

Nothing in God's world is evil.
It is what is done with it.
Respect nuclear energy.
Use it with wisdom.
It will then be allowed its proper place
in your world.
No more, and no less.

The issue is carelessness,
greed, inconsideration,
not nuclear power.
*It is human power that is the issue—
the misuse of human power—
and fear.*
The fear that there is not enough.
Nuclear material is being used as a tool
to fill the pockets of many.

Greed is the toxic waste of deep fear.

What comes to you as dioxin
has come to you in the past as other poison,
as serpentine invasion, perhaps,
or as war, or pestilence.
Dioxin is a modern mode of negativity
and should be treated as such.

Where you, yourselves, are aware
of consciousness creating things
you are then empowered by this wisdom
to bless, to cleanse and to heal.
Yes, even your earth.

Pray for the earth that is afflicted.
Offer those who are suffering
tenderness, love, understanding,
compassion, blessing, healing.
You have yet to realize the power
that you hold within your own consciousness
to alter all things to Light.

See it all with love
and it will be disempowered.

On government:

Governments were never designed
to govern the Light and the soul process
of those who inhabit a country.
All governing bodies, without exception,
have become monstrously out of proportion
to the needs of the people
they were originally formed to serve.

It is time for a universal government.
Let the bonds of nationalistic resistance and illusion
be dissolved, and let all humanity join together
in the recognition of the Oneness
that is the true reality.
Shout it in the streets.

The governments in existence now
were formulated when humankind
was in kindergarten.
It is time to allow those who at least have graduated
from high school (not to mention those
who have entered college in this illusion)
to formulate government
of a much more mature outlook.
Regardless of who sits at the head,
each country is run by the Divine Presence.

**What aspects of consciousness
could produce such a horror
as the Holocaust?**

The expression, "We are all responsible"
is quite right, you know.

It is time you all look within yourselves
to find where you possess such cruelty,
might hold such prejudice, or feel superior,
though you would never act on it.
These judgements could in many many ways
create an atrocity
even though they remain on an intellectual level
or an emotional level that may be buried
from your conscious mind.

In one way or another
everyone contributed to those times,
though one certainly was not there
herding the victims together.
Each one of you, with few exceptions,
entertains the same focuses of consciousness
that, in their exaggerated degree,
brought about that circumstance.

It is a deep learning process.
If it is used as such
those who were physically destroyed
contributed a tremendous gift of love.

There are many, individually and in groups, who are sacrificing their lives very much like those souls in the Holocaust have done, and it seems that the attention needs to be drawn now to more current events in order to allow the lessons to remain clear. Is it not time to focus on the heroism, the sacrifice, the love and the God within each one *now?*

It is much easier to point the finger to the past and say "Look at that!" rather than to say "I must look around me now." For as you see such happenings in the present moment, you will have to do something about them. Monuments are dedicated to frozen thought. They teach as a frame of reference but they also tend to freeze into immobility the constant process of unfoldment. Lessons must be learned and relinquished or perhaps, better said, learned and trusted. We honor the past by honoring the present.

**Will there be
a major international war again?**

The question is unanswerable as asked
not because I would deny you anything
that I am privy to, but because
there are seeds of Light that have been planted.
There is a powerful movement afoot
and you are all part of it.
Wars, like earthquakes, do not just happen.
They are created for purposes
that go far beyond political lines of difference.

As beings of Light and God
you must speak in that nature.
You must celebrate love
but you must first believe in it yourselves.
Therefore, you must test it, challenge it.
You must investigate love
until you know there is no other way to exist.
Once you have found that solid truth,
you will plant your feet there.
You will deny violence and darkness
and you will join God
in the task of healing the earth.

When you look at another person with love
you create what you might term miracles.
For Light expands, and as Light expands
darkness is transformed.

Do not despair.
Hearts are opening.
Truth is being heard more and more.
Courage is building.
There are already enough of you
to say "no" to such destruction.
You have already begun to do so.

On child abuse and torture:

Abuse of any kind is an abuse against God.
There is no way in heaven or earth
that I can say to you
that the abuse and torture of children,
or anyone else, is acceptable.

This is an appalling circumstance in human terms—
not to be tolerated. But let us look beyond that,
not with complacency, but with compassion
and with deep faith in the wisdom of each soul.

What is to be learned from this experience,
not only by the child, but by the parents as well?
Often a child who has been abused
and has even lost its life to abuse
has given a gift
of great love and sacrifice to the parents
if they are willing to receive this gift.

Souls experiencing such abuse chose it
for reasons that are known only to them
and their advisors, their guides.
They will emerge more lighted, more aware
of the meaning of darkness,
more determined and more empowered
to alter that darkness within themselves.

It is quite impossible for you
to see things as God sees them.
Leave your judgements
in the hands of God.
Leave your horror and outrage where it is.
These issues need to be addressed
in your human world.

On abortion:

I think that abortion is a melting pot for a lot of other issues. One must be fully aware of every act in one's life, the act of conception no less than the act of abortion. But when, after profound prayer and consideration, there is a need to terminate a pregnancy, it is not an unforgivable act. If it is done with willingness to learn, it becomes a useful act.

Remember, I am speaking from the world of spirit and I know that no soul is ever destroyed. I know that when a soul chooses to be born, it will be born. *The soul is wise and would not inhabit a body if it were not to come to term.*

There are Divine Laws that go so far beyond the human consciousness that it is difficult to make a statement that says at one level of awareness, "It's perfectly all right," and at another, "You really need to give deep thought to it," and at still another, "Perhaps you shouldn't have done it at all." Nothing in your human world is absolutely wrong.

Should one feel guilt? No. Concern? Yes. Responsibility? Absolutely, as well as compassion and willingness to see the need that speaks behind that unfortunate act.

Why has this pregnancy been allowed to take place? For what are you really longing? Why have you placed yourself in the posture of conceiving without being able, or allowing yourself, to receive the fruits of that conception?

In any manner it is perceived, it is a loss. You have either lost your heart and have entered into an act of conception that had no meaning, or you are in some way denying your own fulfillment.

Yet, if this act is used for growth,
if it opens the way for you to find your own meaning,
your own needs, your own truth and beingness,
then it is a gift.

On capital punishment:

No human being, by the command of God,
has the right to take the life of another.
The soul is not killed, of course.
It is released.
But that is a different matter.
When one has built a structure of human life
then no one, without severely handicapping himself,
can take that life away.

Does killing a murderer, thus causing another murder,
compensate in the consciousness of the soul?
I think not.
There is a need for deep understanding
of the sacredness of every individual.

When, in the course of human experience,
it has seemed necessary
for the preservation of an ideal, a cause, or a life,
that another life be taken,
this does not in any way diminish
the seriousness of that act
but it does add mitigating circumstances.

The more expanded the awareness,
the more responsible one becomes.
Certainly, if awareness is not there,
then the death of another is not as heavy a burden.
It is only within the self that one can know
where awareness truly is.
The depth of consciousness creates the next life
and the next. Remember always
that cause-and-effect is one's own creation.

The moment that the Light is turned on
in the closets of inner darkness
then that Light will forever burn.
Person by person, all will leave the ranks
of public executioner
and there will be no one then to do the work.

Envision a world where everyone says,
"I will not kill."
Do you know
what peace and beauty will descend? ❈

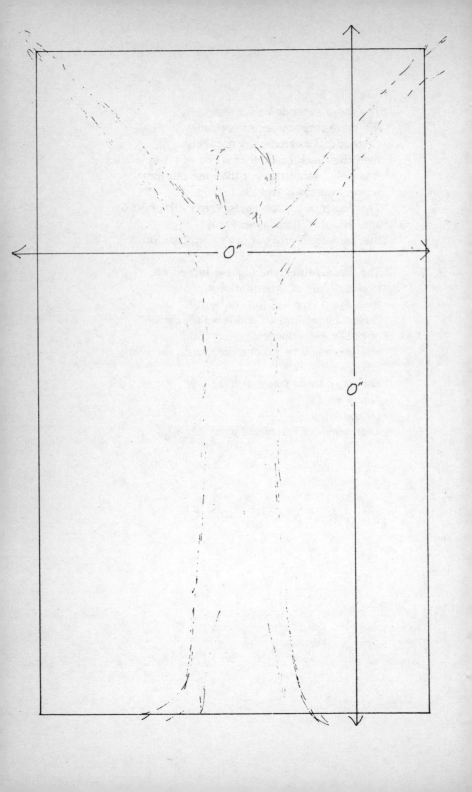

14
Beyond Planet Earth

The pattern of a small world
hurtling endlessly through space
does not quite fit the reality.

You are on the borderline
between all things and you are,
at the same moment, all things.

You are where I am.
I am where you are.
And the physical dimensions
of depth and height and width
have no reality at all.
If you were to remove
the spectacles of human limitation,
you and I would face each other
in perfect equality. ❀

As Beings of Light, you have free passage
wherever in God's universe
your particular consciousness will allow,
to the worlds beyond the physical.

Let us assume that you, a Being of Light,
no longer has a need to be physical.
You have left behind the illusion of illusion
and you are quite free
to expand and explore and create.
The choice is yours.
You may enter into other galaxies,
other realms of consciousness
that are more compatible to your being.
You see, when you do not have a physical body,
there are many planets open to your habitation.
It does not matter how cold it is, does it?
It is truly a remarkable feeling of freedom.

You are free to inhabit wherever it is you feel drawn,
wherever it is your curiosity takes you.
You see lights, colors that are far more brilliant
than you can perceive
while you are in the human atmosphere.
You hear sounds that are exquisite,
beyond comprehension.
This is not a fairytale.
This is like taking off earmuffs and hearing,
taking off boots
and feeling the warm sand on your feet.

Your world offers you these promises
but you have yet to hear them as promises.

Only a small portion of the soul consciousness
exists in human form at a time.
The personality, as it is experienced,
is a bit of the soul that is not yet blended
with the Light.
The areas of resistance become human.

The less necessary the human experience becomes,
the less stern the schoolroom
and the more of a sweet kiss life can be. ⚘

How can you know,
as long as there is a portion of you
that is human,
what is perfect and what is not?
Perhaps in the Divine Plan,
which *is* perfect, a dusting of human imperfection
is absolutely perfect for the moment.

Was Christ so dusted?

Indeed. There were moments of blinding glory.
There were moments of absolute knowing.
But there were also moments of cloudiness,
moments of forgetting, and these
were anguish for Him.

The very nature of human form,
though it be donned by one who is committed
to the life of truth, such as He was,
the physical body itself dusts the consciousness.

**It's been said that Krishna and others who used the
human body were not fully human.
Is it possible that anybody like that
can walk the earth?**

It is possible to don a physical body.
It is not possible
to enter into the drama of human experience.
There is a subtle difference there.
Christ acknowledged the value for Him
and His experience and His message
and His teaching and His devotion
to enter into the physical human experience.
There are many who have not. There are many
who put on physical clothing for a moment,
for a year, for what seems to be
a reasonable lifetime,
without truly experiencing humanness.
That's all right too.
There are beings that materialize,
as it were, in the midst of a crowded subway
or stand on a street corner,
suddenly there to help, to teach, to guide,
and then to vanish—these are such.
They know no humanness.

Emmanuel, what is your world like?

Well, if I were to take you on a tour
I would delight in showing you brilliance of color,
sweetness of air,
delight of perception in all manner.
I would offer you
streets of safety, beauty and softness,
aromas of incredible wonder.
All things that are contained in physical promise
in your world come to fulfillment in mine.

Do you have honeysuckle there?

It is the essence of honeysuckle
and it is absorbed not only through the nostrils
but through every portion of who I am.

You can begin to touch my world
even while you are in your own
by allowing yourself to experience without boundaries.
For example, when you eat a meal, taste your food
not only through your tastebuds,
but see it in its beauty,
hear it (it has a sound), see the vibrant life,
the gift of love that food is offering to you.
Let your body absorb the light and delight of it.
Eat slowly, compassionately. Eat with awareness
and you will begin to see what my world is like.
It is essentially the same, but so much more.

The mind can stretch
in an in-turning endless universe
as well as an expanding endless universe.

In this way, the frame of reference
is within your grasp.
As one goes deeper,
for example, in the physical sciences,
to the worlds
within the worlds within the worlds,
there is a stretching of the consciousness
that goes beyond all things.

The curve of the earth
pulls human thoughts into its orbit.
What then of "straight" thinking?

Thoughts of God
would be straight thinking,
clarity and perception
beyond the bend of the earth,
whatever that means to you.
This may have varied meanings
for varied levels of consciousness
but it will tend to release your thoughts
from the circular motion
around the earth.

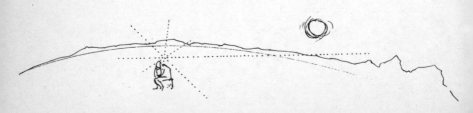

**Does the soul we know
as Jesus the Christ
continue to live
perhaps in other realms?**

What an interesting question!
First we must begin by evolving
through the physicality of your galaxies
and into the greater realities that rest beyond
what even now seems so remote to you
through the magnification of telescopes.

There are planets, certainly, that hold life
of every conceivable consciousness.
Yet much above and beyond that there are realms
that go *far* beyond the physical.
Physicality is but the smallest of dimensions
in the eternal greatness.

There are those realms where Christ walks
even at this moment in Light and truth,
in joy and wholeness, and in deep and profound
regard and worship.
Yet, I tell you this—again not to confound you
but there is no other way to say this—
there are comingled
within your planet and its physicality
other realities.

The greater reality
which you have all touched in meditation and prayer,
truly coexists in the same space
where your cars and your boats,
your water and your parks
and your rain and yourselves also sit.
In that expanded reality
that shares all eternity with you
Christ is alive and well
and walks among you.

We all exist in many realities at once.
It is impossible to place them geographically.
Placing them in awareness
will bring you closer to the truth
for one can focus one's attention
on minutiae and swear that nothing
exists in the world but one grain of sand.
One can also focus
on a broader and broader spectrum
until you are fully aware
of walking hand in hand with Christ,
constantly, throughout all of your daily activities.
It is not geographical.
It is truth.

**Is there life
on other planets?**

Yes. Teeming and abundant.

You are all loved and protected,
not only by us in the plane of consciousness
where I exist, but by many
who are in planes of consciousness
that are similar to your own.
These beings have existed in your world
and have grown to live in other spheres
where consciousness is higher and more evolved.
This is their choice.

There have been many times
in the past history of the earth
when humanity has learned that it is not alone.
Then that knowledge has been dispersed
because the Divine purpose of such communication
was fulfilled.

There is a time coming
when intergalactic communication
will become a part of everyday existence.
This will not be until the hearts
of those who are incarnated on your planet
are ready to receive that guidance,
not in a dependent childlike way,
but in the way of brotherhood.

**Does life elsewhere
take the same forms
as it does here?**

Oh, no. There are 'elsewheres'
of greater or lesser awareness.
These are steps, stages.
This is not the only planet
that God has created for your schoolroom.
You go from here to many, many others
that are more blissful, more enlightened,
more exciting, more expanded, more creative
and more filled with love.
There, you see
you needn't be afraid to graduate at all.

**Who are our nearest neighbors
in the universe
and what will be
our first contact?**

We are, and the contact has already been made.
Oh, I know you are speaking of extraterrestrial beings.
Contact has already been made regardless
of how you translate extraterrestrial.

This will become more apparent
as the willingness to hear beyond the expected
is developed in your human community.
There are already those who claim to be in contact
with visitors from other planets.
There has been a reluctance to hear this.
It is all too mysterious.
Quite truthfully, the time is not yet right
for acceptance of this, for we are still involved
in awakening the ability to expand
to the realm of spirit, to the world of God.

My personal reaction to the visitation
from other physically manifested beings
is that it would be a distraction at this time.
It has happened and will continue to happen
as emissaries reach
across the illusion of time and space,
for ultimately, my dears,
all is one, all is here, all is now.

As you consider this matter in the future,
be aware of the reality that exists
beyond time and space and you will see
that the question has meaning
only as you rest in the physical world.

Souls that exist in other galaxies
are very much like you.
Though there may be great wisdom
in the guidance received
from the expanded consciousness
of these evolved beings,
there is also sometimes error.

Divine Law is Divine Law.
Everyone must stumble.
Even those who have advanced far beyond
the earth's consciousness.
Do not require perfection
of yourself or of other beings.

**Please tell us
what Planet Earth looks like
from a distance.**

I see Light.
I see consciousness.
I see waves upon waves
of prayer and supplication,
of pain and of joy
leaving your earth.
There is a constant flow
of the consciousness of longing
away from your earth,
a constant flow of healing
towards it.
There is continuing communication
which I perceive in waves of Light.

A Parting Word

You are lights.
Wherever you are is lighted.
You are never in darkness.
You are only approaching darkness.
You are never in death.
You are only approaching death
for when death is entered
it is life.
For you are alive.

Therefore, once you have found yourself
you are infinitely safe
for you are always who you are.
Ultimately, when you return Home
to be received by God,
you will welcome yourself
with love and understanding.

Glossary

There needs to be almost a tongue-in-cheek
sobriety about the world that you inhabit, if only to
realize that what seems to be so solidly cemented
in immutable reality is, in the expanded view, a
delightful illusion.

If a concept is limited in any manner, the limitation
is for identification, to hold it so it can be seen.
The purpose of this glossary, then, is to shake the
meaning loose from its frozen place, rather than to
give a word a workable definition. Each human
being, each consciousness able to formulate a
meaning to a word, needs to be aware of where
that definition is rigid and confining. It is the task
of each soul to do its own inner glossary research.

Play with this glossary. Then shake your personal
glossary up and tumble it about a bit, and you will
see that you are already where you are seeking to
go. It is a matter of definition...yours.

Antimatter: Through the looking glass. To go to the farthest possible extreme of denial of what is here, and yet it is still here.

Beautiful: A word whose meaning needs to be allowed to flow to the unexpected.

Body: The body is a shell formulated by your own consciousness in order to enclose the spirit so that you can complete the tasks undertaken in a given life.

Community: This concept needs to go beyond walls and streets and houses and national borders.

Eternity: The word 'eternity' could stand a little expansion.

Grace: Grace is the fabric of God's Consciousness. It is eternal love. Everything is Grace.

Growth: Willingness to change, to learn, to experience, to expand, celebrate, rejoice, worship, and ultimately to surrender. Growth is more than physical growth or emotional learning. It is a readiness to explore one's own inner reality, especially the darker areas. Ask who you would like to become. That is growth.

Humanness: Humanness is not a hard and fixed armoring, but a most porous and flexible reality.

Humility: To be human and to rest in a state of humanness consciously, openly, willingly.

Illusion: All reality that is not pure Light and Consciousness is illusion.

Karma: The text of your journey through this particular lifetime.

Life: Life is for growth. It has no other purpose.

Love: The moment love has definition, it loses its power. If one defines love by its actions, one displaces love. One knows love by living without it. One finds love by realizing one has lost it. One loses love by losing the Self. One can find love by finding the Self, or even by seeking the Self.

Matter: Matter is consciousness.

Oneness: Oneness is expansion, and in that expansion, I am you and you are me and together we are Love.

Relationship: The heart looking for a home. The yearning looking for a place to be.

Soul, Spirit, Consciousness: These terms might be seen as synonymous. As I use them, a being is eternal consciousness and this is housed in what humanity considers a soul, which is, of course, the realm of spirit. Their absolute definition is impossible.

Space: Space and time meet at the point where consciousness is ready to relinquish itself.

Symbology: To take something and compress it. Language is the most obvious example of symbology. There is a remarkable number of misses in communication, rather than direct hits.

Symbols: Everything in human existence. The symbol becomes the antithesis of itself the moment it is frozen in your conceptualization.

Teaching: Not a didactic act, but a sense of being. This beingness needs to allow for its own expansion.

Thought: A vital function in human reality as you experience it while you are still in your human body. When you are free of that limited use of thought, it then becomes the internal expression of the patterns of your entire being.

Time: A container, a form. Time is a resting place. When consciousness cannot abide infinite reality, then it clings to time. The essence of time, therefore, is consciousness. Time is being. It is both the most minute reality and the most expanded, and its moment is eternity.

Truth: Truth *is*. No one has authored truth. Each one expresses it in his or her own way.

The World: A learning situation, often a reflection of struggle.

A Taste
of Absolute Freedom
and Peace
(Emmanuel's spiritual exercises)

251

Exercises:
Some ways and means of expansion

These exercises must go according to your ability at the moment of use. Initially, the greatest struggle is just to sit down and acknowledge that a time of silence can be beneficial. Then you can move through greater depths or in varying directions as, for instance, a practice for self-love, or a specific meditation to find the eternality of the Self, and so on.

Having decided to sit with the intent to release judgement of self, to go beneath fear and to find the citadel of Oneness within each human being, the next step is as follows: whatever practice, at any given time, calls you, adopt it. Whatever format lends itself to your needs, accept it. Be willing to change practices when your needs change. There is nothing more obstructive to the goals of meditation than rigidity or insistence upon any particular format. These exercises are open for picking and choosing where the spirit delights.

The purposes of such exercises are unique and individual. The ultimate purpose, of course, is to be free, to lift beyond the confines of human experience and to taste, just for a moment, the flavor of absolute freedom and peace.

So let us begin. The authorship of these practices is not mine. These exercises have been devised and formulated over the centuries by many spirits, beings of Light both physical and non-physical. I offer them to you as such.

Those who have used them can extoll their virtues for self-development, as well as the pleasure of such practices as they lead to introspection and self-finding.

1. **How to love yourself
   and others.**

To begin to practice loving, it would be well to start with yourself. Beyond that, the sharing with another will be as gently flowing as the sweetest kiss of spring. So, let me offer this to you as a bit of homework.

Stand before your mirror, alone, paper and pencil at hand. Draw a line down the center of the page. On the left hand side of the page write, "This is what I accept about myself." Notice I did not say 'love'. On the other side write, "This is what I do not accept about myself." Then hold an honest and open discourse with that image in the mirror.

See yourself on many different levels of reality, from the highest to the lowest, from the most mature to the most immature, from the sweetest to the harshest, from the most loving to the angriest you have ever been.

Allow yourself to experience the love, the compassion, the hate, the rage, the jealousy and the sacrifice. Begin to take note of how you judge your judging, how you disbelieve your lovingness, how you take pride in your self-censuring.

None of this is to be done harshly. No. No. There has been enough of that. But with an eye to truth. The shame you feel when you truly love yourself is heartbreaking. You have come to learn love. You cannot love another more than you love yourself. You cannot love God more than you love another.

Hold a dialogue with yourself in the mirror for at least ten minutes—more if you like (you can spend hours if it pleases you), but at least ten minutes— then close your eyes and see yourself bathed in the radiant light of love. Accept it. Let it come through your pores. You are bathed in love every minute of every day, for you *are* love.

**2. A mode of tuning in
    to your inner text.**

Take a moment out of each hour during your day and ask yourself, "What do I want now?" "What decisions am I making now?" "Who am I now?", and "What am I doing now?"

This practice focuses an inner awareness. It is a tuning in to your very essence that will give you the freedom of choice at 360 degrees.

**3. Dealing
    with fear.**

It is in focusing on the difficult that fear is made master. It is experiencing the easy that gives you the stability to move through the fear.

So, begin to image what it will be like to live without fear. Start by envisioning yourself walking down a simple street. Go from one block to the next and see how often fear is there. Fear can be identified not only as terror, but as resistance, as limitation, as hesitancy, as weariness or distrust.

Next, envision some simple, simple act done completely without fear (you will tackle the complicated ones later). Do this five minutes a day.

4. How to refresh yourself.

Go into the inner self, the 'me-ness.' Find that self and breathe into it a moment.

Ask that me what is making it tired right now. "What would you rather be doing now? What are you sitting on? What are you denying?" (Human bodies don't need nearly as much rest as you think they do. What they need is release. What they need is permission to express. What they need is their free-flowing passion.)

Ninety nine times out of a hundred when you are tired it is not because of what you have done, but what didn't you do that you wanted to. So ask yourself these questions.

And next time, if you can do so without destruction, allow yourself to do what you would like to do. That is not self-indulgence as you have all been taught. That is self-respect.

5. Making your own acquaintance.

Go within into your silence. Envision yourself entering a room. No one is in there but you. Suddenly, across the room, you perceive yourself as you *really* are, in your inner beauty. Allow yourself to make your acquaintance, tenderly, lovingly.

Now, take yourself by the hand. Bring yourself
back with you. Keep yourself close to you for the
rest of your life. That being you have just met has
been waiting for you to notice them throughout
your entire life. And once you have noticed, once
you have learned who you are (and it will take
many such exercises; I urge you to do them at least
once a day) you will begin to realize that it matters
very little what anyone else thinks. And won't *that*
set you free?

6. Re-perceiving the self.

For ten minutes each day see yourselves as truly
God-like beings with the delicious task of
spreading Light wherever you are.

See yourselves as unabashedly giving love and
delight, as smiling, as believing in peace and in joy
and in the absence of pain.

Try it. You will find that it is the most contagious
thing you have ever caught.

7. Discovering your task in life.

What do you do the best? What gives you the
greatest sense of fulfillment? That is where your
task lies.

The heart speaks not only through prayer and
meditation, but it also speaks through desire—pure,
simple human desire.

8. A way to awaken memories of 'past' lives.

In order to do this, find the one who is most dear to you and at a time of mutual availability sit facing each other comfortably. Touch your hands and close your eyes and allow, without a word spoken, a vision to come.

Nothing must be forced. Trust the greater reality. It is far wiser and far more creative than your conscious mind. Then, after a bit of time, share the image. I am quite sure that this will bring you a surprising degree of verification that both of you have had mutual past experiences.

9. Expanding the self.

Close your eyes. Concentrate on the forefinger of
your right hand. Experience its dimension. You are
familiar with that finger. You know its size, shape,
how it feels.

Now extend your awareness of that finger as far as
it will go, as far as you are able to feel comfortable,
still feeling "yes, that is my finger."

Now expand your finger beyond that familiar
feeling. You notice that the self fills that finger-
space too, pushing out the boundaries of the
familiar without loss of self.

That is what you are all about, pushing out
boundaries without loss of self, extending into the
Greater Self through that process, being willing to
go beyond the known into the unknown, which
instantaneously becomes the known when you
have entered.

10. Erasing your physical boundaries.

Close your eyes and envision the outline of your physical body as though it were drawn with a very dark pencil. Be faithful to the shape of your body.

Having outlined yourself, you have identified clearly the personality-ego structure.

Now, envision a large eraser, and allow it to begin to erase the lines of the physical body (some portions may prove more stubborn than others and this information will be useful for later self-inquiry).

When you reach the top of your head, do an exceptionally thorough job of erasing that area. Let whatever happens happen. Give it time.

Allow the consciousness of Self to expand.

You have now challenged the illusion of human physical experience. Depending on how courageous you have been in erasing, you have permitted yourself to expand far beyond that line of physical identity.

11. Staying in the Now.

There really *is* an Eternal Now. Here is an effortless way to reach it (effortless because one must breathe).

Close your eyes and focus your consciousness on this moment. Become aware of your breathing. Observe its ebb and flow. Now, as you breathe, inhale into the next instant of your existence. As you exhale, breathe out all that ever was. Inhale again into the future. Exhale all the past.

Consciously follow your breath. Let each exhalation free you. Let each inhalation bring you to the moment of the present. That is all there is. Practice this for a while.

Now, as you reach the apex of your inhalation, pause a moment, not forcing, allowing the natural pause, then exhale. More and more now, as you touch that space between inhalation and exhalation, let yourself rest there (again without stress). And you are touching the Eternal Now.

As you practice this, you will find the space between inhalation and exhalation broadening and becoming your place of habitation.

No future. No past. Just being.

12. A spot check.

As you walk through your day make note of those moments when
  A. you stop your own loving
  B. you believe you are not worthy of love.

Epilogue

To work with, to digest and assimilate Emmanuel's viewpoints over a period of time, over the five years, in fact, that it has taken to assemble this book, has been a process which Emmanuel discussed in a meditation with those of us involved, Pat, Roland, Ram Dass and myself.

He said, "It has been necessary to hone, to design and redesign, to poke, prod and probe in order to accomplish not just the publication of the book, but the purposes within each one of you as to the worthiness of your contributions, and, indeed, the truth of the entire matter. As you have worked, you dear sweet beings of forgotten Light, you have found in the words, in the phrases and within the entire concept itself, the courage to believe once more in many things that you thought you had forgotten. Having heard these things, initially you thought you could not bring yourselves to trust in them.

None of you are strangers to the heights of aspiration, but have come again and again, fully determined to climb the ultimate mountain. And each time there has been detour, there has been pause, there has, in short, been fear—fear from the forgetting of the 'who' that you are that has come to do the 'what.'

Now that 'what' is not of any importance at all once the 'who' is recognized. You all know this but it bears repeating as do most things, since the human memory is very short. Even though it determines to hold to something that it instantaneously knows to be truth, the clouding of the memory is simply part of the process of human experience. In this work there has been an opportunity again and again to open the doors to what you have forgotten.

Let us, then, relinquish memory and allow experience to flow. There is nothing to cling to. There is no necessity to remember anything, but only to *be* and that requires absolute faith. For in the beingness nothing is in control. There is only Is-ness, which is the absolute safety of God."

In working with the 'what', this book, we have indeed been constantly reminded of the truth of the entire matter. The courage to believe once more in the many things we had forgotten was reinforced and reinforced again. Repetition has dissolved, for me, many of the fears which had inhibited the flow of experience.

I urge you also to use this book repeatedly, to work with it, to open the doors again and again, and let Emmanuel lead you ever closer to recognizing your eternal safety.

I am so deeply grateful to Emmanuel and I thank him from the bottom of my heart.

Judith Stanton